CIVILIAN R
WORKBOOK

OPERATION: <u>CIVILIAN</u> RÉSUMÉ
4-Battlefield Phases to a Targeted <u>Civilian</u> Résumé

Bruce Benedict Major, U.S. Army, Retired

Pre-Publication Review completed on February 19, 2014. DoD clearance and case number 14-S-0670. DIA case number 14-009. Cleared for open publication.

Disclaimer Statement: The views express in the manuscript are those of the author and do not reflect the official policy or position of the U.S. Government, the Department of Defense, or any of its components.

Copyright © 2013 Bruce Benedict, Battlefield Résumés, LLC

All rights reserved.

ISBN-13: 978-1500981327
ISBN-10: 150098132X

DEDICATION

This workbook is dedicated to those men and women who work for and support the Department of Defense.

"Duty, Honor, Country.
Those three hallowed words reverently dictate what you ought to be, what you can be, what you will be. They are your rallying points: to build courage when courage seems to fail; to regain faith when there appears to be little cause for faith; to create hope when hope becomes forlorn."
(General Douglas MacArthur).

CONTENTS

	Acknowledgments	i
	Preface	1
1	Chapter 1: The Battlefield	Pg 5
2	Chapter 2: Battlefield Definitions	Pg 9
3	Chapter 3: Intelligence Preparation of the Battlefield	Pg 13
4	Chapter 4: Phase Line Describe	Pg 18
5	Chapter 5: Phase Line Analyze	Pg 26
6	Chapter 6: Phase Line Evaluate	Pg 42
7	Chapter 7: Phase Line Target	Pg 50
8	Chapter 8: The Enemy's Perspective of You	Pg 60
9	Chapter 9: Rehearsal	Pg 71
10	Chapter 10: Mission Accomplished	Pg 96
A	Appendix A: Rehearsal Answers	Pg 100
B	Appendix B: Action Verbs	Pg 121
C	Appendix C: Targeted Verbs	Pg 129
D	Appendix D: Competencies	Pg 134
	Glossary	Pg 140
	Index	Pg 145

ACKNOWLEDGMENTS

I would like to thank my family and friends for their support and cooperation in helping me develop this workbook.

PREFACE

WARNING ORDER

Prepare your Civilian Résumé for Battle

"TO SECURE OURSELVES AGAINST DEFEAT LIES IN OUR OWN HANDS, BUT THE OPPORTUNITY OF DEFEATING THE ENEMY IS PROVIDED BY THE ENEMY HIMSELF."
(SUN TZU, THE ART OF WAR)

What is a Warning Order? As described in Joint Publication 1-02, a Warning Order is:

1. A preliminary notice of an order or action, which is to follow.
2. A crisis action planning directive that initiates the development and evaluation of Courses of Action by a supported commander and requests that a commander's estimate of the situation be submitted.
3. A planning directive that describes the situation, allocates forces and resources, establishes command relationships, provides other initial planning guidance and initiates subordinate unit mission planning.

The US Army Field Manual 5-0, defines a Warning Order as the following: "A Warning Order helps subordinate units and staffs prepare for new missions. They increase subordinates' planning time, provide details of the impending operation and detail events that accompany preparation and execution. The amount of detail a Warning Order includes depends on the information and time available when it is issued and the information subordinate commanders need for proper planning and preparation."

This preface is labeled - Warning Order - to clarify that your mission is about to begin. This is literally a warning that you are about to **embrace in a battle** for only the well prepared. As with the military version of Warning Orders (or perhaps to introduce you to this way of thinking), I too am putting you on notice that you now have a mission to accomplish. You need to start your mission preparation immediately in order to develop the appropriate Operations Order and weapon.

My idea in preparing this 4-Battlefield Phases to a Targeted Résumé was to design a workbook for those with a military or Defense Department background. Ironically, most books are hundreds of pages long but of little use to the novice résumé writer. Such books become too lengthy to read and only lead to confusion. In this workbook, 4-Battlefield Phases to a Targeted Résumé, the primary thrust was to design a workbook that everyone could read and understand, while using this training to enhance your own experience in résumé development. There are no secrets to résumé writing, however, there are specific principles to which you must adhere in order to secure an interview and ultimately a job.

This workbook is meant to be read from front to back. This method of reading is encouraged in order to obtain the true context from which the

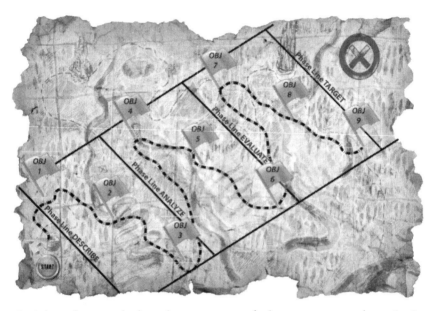

principles of targeted résumés are presented. As we progress through the workbook the associations with military terminology, lexicon and methodology are critical and, therefore, require a thorough understanding. The only way to reach this pinnacle of understanding is to read this material sequentially, ensuring you completely understand the principles by which competitive defense contractor résumés are built.

The formula that I have developed to help train you in building a targeted résumé is based on the military's use of the Intelligence Preparation of the Battlefield, otherwise known as "IPB." Intelligence Preparation of the Battlefield is what the military uses to prepare for battle. The Army explains it in detail within Field Manual 34-130 and describes Intelligence Preparation of the Battlefield as "the systematic, continuous process of analyzing the threat and environment in a specific geographic area. Intelligence Preparation of the Battlefield is designed to support the staff estimate and military decision-making process (otherwise known as "MDMP"). Most intelligence requirements are generated as a result of the Intelligence Preparation of the Battlefield process and its interrelation with the military decision making process."

For those readers who are not familiar with military terminology or methodology, please do not worry. Although the term Intelligence Preparation of the Battlefield and other military acronyms are used throughout this workbook, great effort and special thought has been taken in describing each as thoroughly as possible. As a matter of fact, after reading this workbook, it is quite possible that you will better understand military methods and terms as it relates to a real battlefield, while associating these activities to a résumé and vacancy announcement. The workbook details the procedures to follow in preparing Intelligence Preparation of the Battlefield for defense contractor related positions, using battlefield illustrations and descriptions while applying the Intelligence Preparation of the Battlefield process for various types of vacancy announcements.

This workbook is intended to serve as a guide for the use of Intelligence Preparation of the Battlefield by military and/or defense department transitioning professionals, defense contractors and federal government employees. It is intended to be a working guide so you can apply the fundamentals of the Intelligence Preparation of the Battlefield process to any and all vacancy announcements, résumés and cover letters.

Please do not interpret any part of this document as limiting your freedom of writing résumés. Also, please do not infer that all résumé writing must be prepared by using Intelligence Preparation of the Battlefield in all situations. However, all defense department professionals should leverage this methodology as presented and tailor their résumé accordingly.

Again, this workbook is written for transitioning veterans and for anyone seeking a defense contracting position. This workbook applies equally from the GS-1/Private (E-1) to the GS-15/Colonel (O-6) level, State/Federal Government and transitioning Active, Reserve and National Guard service members, as well as defense contractors. This workbook may also prove helpful to others who would like to apply for positions requiring a SECRET or TOP SECRET clearance in the federal government or defense contracting.

This workbook is written from the author's point of view and experiences that he has witnessed. Bruce entered the military immediately after high school, moved over 16 times with the US Army all over the world. He deployed numerous times to the Middle East and retired after serving 21 years. He has experienced and observed the anxiety caused by leaving the military and transitioning into the civilian workforce. He personally believes that associating common military methodologies and terminology to the civilian résumé lessens the transition anxiety and stress.

Bruce hopes you enjoy reading this workbook and wishes you the best in developing tailored and targeted résumés, as well as the successful "battles" you will win by using this program.

CHAPTER 1

THE BATTLEFIELD

"ENGAGE PEOPLE WITH WHAT THEY EXPECT; IT IS WHAT THEY ARE ABLE TO DISCERN AND CONFIRMS THEIR PROJECTIONS. IT SETTLES THEM INTO PREDICTABLE PATTERNS OF RESPONSE, OCCUPYING THEIR MINDS WHILE YOU WAIT FOR THE EXTRAORDINARY MOMENT - THAT WHICH THEY CANNOT ANTICIPATE."
(SUN TZU, THE ART OF WAR)

The Battlefield is a necessary evil. The Battlefield is a treacherous place where two opponents come clashing together, competing, ironically, for similar thing (ownership of the land itself), but for different purposes.

In order to claim the battlefield as your own, you must *analyze* the battlefield better than the enemy; you must *evaluate* the battlefield better than the enemy; and, you must *develop* a better strategy and *implement* that strategy better than the enemy. Additionally, more times than not, one opponent is already occupying the ground when the battle occurs. This opponent is said to be in a defensive posture/position and is known to have the advantage. The enemy, in a defensive position, assumes the advantage because of their assumed familiarity with the terrain and length of time they have had to prepare for battle. Ultimately, the opponent who better prepares will inevitably defeat the less prepared opponent.

In writing a résumé, you must assume that the hiring manager wrote the vacancy announcement. Because of this, you must also assume that the hiring manager is more familiar with the nuances and requirements of the vacancy announcement than you. Therefore, you must identify the hiring manager as being in a defensive posture and, therefore, must label this person as your "Enemy." Due to the enemy's current defensive position, you are at an immediate disadvantage because you are unfamiliar with the battlefield. Therefore, you must spend sufficiently more time preparing for battle than the enemy. You must analyze the battlefield against the terrain and environment, while analyzing, evaluating and developing a strategy to defeat the enemy.

In this workbook, you will identify the following critical components of battlefield résumé writing:

1. **"The Battlefield"**_{TM} is the <u>vacancy announcement.</u>
2. **"A Battle"**_{TM} is <u>each vacancy announcement you apply to</u>.
3. **"Operations Order/Weapon"**_{TM} is <u>your résumé</u>.
4. **"The Enemy/High Value Target"**_{TM} is the <u>person who will review your résumé</u> against the vacancy announcement requirements. In this workbook, this person is referred to as the hiring manager, selecting official or recruiter.
5. **"Your Mission"**_{TM} is to <u>acquire/occupy the key terrain</u>.
6. **"The War"**_{TM} is the <u>culmination of all battles</u>.
7. **"Win the War"**_{TM} is <u>being hired for the job you applied to</u>.
8. **"Other Soldiers"**_{TM} describes your <u>competition or the list of other applicants</u> applying to the same vacancy announcement.
9. **"Key Terrain"**_{TM} is the <u>invitation to be interviewed</u>.

The battlefield is the one common piece of ground that all other Soldiers can see, analyze and evaluate, against which they can tailor a strategy. They must also correctly predict the Enemy's actions on the battlefield, by correctly identifying the Enemy's intent when writing the vacancy announcement and/or interpreting the requirements of the vacancy announcement. They must identify subtle patterns of the environment such as key words and phrases used in the vacancy announcement, as well as patterns/signatures throughout the battlefield/vacancy announcement in order to transform the battlefield/vacancy announcement into a malleable advantage greater to them than their opponents. This, my friends, is the strategy of all battles.

"Other Soldiers" is the description given to the list of other applicants applying for the same position. All other Soldiers analyze and evaluate the battlefield/vacancy announcement; yet one opponent inevitably develops a better strategy, better identifies patterns and better identifies key objectives than the other Soldiers, ultimately winning the battle.

> **NOTE:** This descriptive comparison by no means is meant to downplay the significance of a true military battlefield and the horrors that occur, but only to lend a common association with transitioning military and

Defense Department personnel to the civilian workforce.

Many transitioning military members have deployed numerous times around the world and, similar to Bruce's experience, have lost close friends and/or family members in those conflicts. Although not as devastating as losing a friend or family member, your transition from the military into the civilian workforce is similarly traumatic and extremely stressful in other ways. Now you must enter an environment unfamiliar to you, unfriendly to your demeanor and experiences. Yet, once confronted with this uninviting environment, most military and/or Defense Department personnel will normally fall back onto our experiences in an attempt to establish a common "mental" understanding of the present.

The stress is tremendous and the uncertainty enormous. It feels as if everyone is counting on us to maintain a high and predictable standard of living, yet no one is there to help you.

Your military experiences, travels and deployments, although stressful, were filled with camaraderie, team support, planning, mission, goals and objectives. Now, unlike our military battlefield experience, you only have yourself to face the enemy and only yourself to face each battle. The pressure is high, you must now accurately analyze and evaluate the enemy's actions independently, without error, to ensure you take care of your family. Ultimately, you feel the burden lies directly on your shoulders and failure is not an option.

As previously mentioned, the vacancy announcement is what you will call "the battlefield," since it is the common ground for which all applicants initially compete for a job. It's the first time in the war that you come face-to-face with the enemy. Since you must assume that the enemy is in a defensive position, you have to associate each movement as "entering terrain that is owned by the enemy." This workbook will walk you through the battlefield, phase line by phase line, calculating each step and accomplishing each objective. Ultimately, if you maneuver accurately, you will take over the key terrain and the High Value Target (also known as the HVT).

Key terrain can be associated with the game "king of the hill" that many of us played as children. All competitors competed to see who could get to the top of the hill before anyone else. The person that reached the hill first had the advantage and a better angle in keeping others from controlling the hill. However, once a person was on top of the hill/key terrain, that person became the focal point for everyone and was now the High Value Target. At that point, the objective was to push the High Value Target off the hill in order to control the hill yourself. This is no different from the battlefield.

Your mission is to obtain control of the key terrain, or in this workbook, we call it "obtaining the interview." However, first you must accurately aim at the High Value Target to ensure you can obtain the key terrain. In this case, the High Value Target is the enemy, or hiring manager. Once you have appropriately targeted and obtained control over the hiring manager/High Value Target by using your tailored and targeted résumé, only then will you be able to take control of the key terrain/interview.

To remain competitive, you must look at each vacancy announcement as a separate battlefield, each having distinctly different key terrain, high value targets, objectives, phase lines, etc. This is no different than writing different operations orders (otherwise known as an OPORD) for each battle.

Here, you must write a different résumé for each vacancy announcement. Think about what would happen if the military always used the same Operations Order for every battle throughout the world. To the enemy, this would be interpreted as ludicrous and a huge vulnerability for the US military. This is no different from a hiring manager who sees your same résumé repeatedly for multiple vacancies, immediately recognizing how generic the résumé is and how little time you spent on developing the résumé. This interpretation infers that your work ethic mirrors the effort spent in writing your résumé. In this instance, using the same résumé (or Operations Order) for each vacancy announcement (or battle) will cause you more harm than good. The Battlefield is the decisive fight and the most prepared opponent will ultimately depart successful.

CHAPTER 2
BATTLEFIELD DEFINITIONS

"THE CLEVER COMBATANT IMPOSES HIS WILL ON THE
ENEMY, BUT DOES NOT ALLOW THE ENEMY'S WILL TO BE
IMPOSED ON HIM."
(SUN TZU, THE ART OF WAR)

To ensure you are immersed into the battlefield, key terms are defined and associated with Intelligence Preparation of the Battlefield terminology to that of vacancy announcement definitions. This is unavoidable in order to prepare you for battle. The following items are key terms that will facilitate your understanding of the 4-Battlefield Phases to a Targeted Résumé process and how to best analyze a defense contractor vacancy announcement as it relates to military doctrine:

Avenue of Approach (AA) ™ – This is the route you choose in which to maneuver through the terrain in order to achieve each objective on the battlefield. Avenues of Approaches are based on the capabilities, opportunities and critical information obtained by analyzing the area of operation (also known as the "AO"). An Avenue of Approach is depicted on the battlefield as a dotted line to each objective.

Area of Operations (AO) ™ – This is the general work and skill area from which information and intelligence are required to permit planning of your successful operation. An example of an Area of Operation is a career area, such as the intelligence career field or the medical career field. The Area of Operation usually consists of multiple vacancies for the same type of position. For example, if you were looking at an Intelligence Analyst vacancy announcement, then the Area of Interest (AI) would be the use of multiple Intelligence Analyst vacancy announcements. Another example would be a Registered Respiratory Therapist vacancy announcement within the medical career field. The Area of Operation includes vacancy announcements from multiple companies and/or organizations that will help in identifying patterns, key words and vacancy requirements.

Course of Action (COA) ₜₘ – This is the tailored strategy, theme or format that you choose based on intelligence gathered from your Area of Operation. Your Course of Action should offer you the best chance of success in achieving your mission.

Decision Point (DP) ₜₘ - The point where you must anticipate making a decision concerning a specific Course of Action. Decision Points are usually associated with vacancy requirements.

Direction of Attack ₜₘ - A specific direction that the main attack or the main body of the force will follow. The Direction of Attack is depicted on a map as shown below. An example of this is when a hiring manager writes a vacancy announcement, often times they will start from the top and describe the position needing filled, then move their way down the page to the applicant requirements for the position. However, as the applicant, your direction of attack should be from the bottom of the vacancy upward. This ensures that you read the vacancy requirements first to confirm you are qualified for the position prior to applying for it (or otherwise known as entering into battle).

Enemy/High Value Target (HVT) ₜₘ – This is the hiring manager and/or Selecting Official who wrote the vacancy announcement and/or who will read your résumé to determine if you deserve an interview. The High Value Target is shown below as a red circle with an X through the middle.

Indicator ₜₘ – An indicator is the evidence of an activity or any characteristic of the Area of Operation that points toward the hiring manager's desired applicant/employee experience. These indicators may influence the hiring manager's selection decision. For example, if an action verb is mentioned repetitively, this is an indicator that the hiring manager wants to see this term in your résumé to describe your work experiences.

Key Terrain ₜₘ – This is the area of ground on the battlefield that provides all participants an advantage in battle. Key terrain is often selected for use as objectives.

Objective ₜₘ – These are critical points/locations on the battlefield that must be reached and accomplished in order to move to the next phase of

the operation. The objective symbol is shown below:

Pattern Analysis ₜₘ – This is when you analyze key terminology and vacancy announcement descriptions and evaluate patterns in the Area of Operation. Pattern analysis leads to the development of your tailored Course of Action strategy.

Phase Lines (PL) ₜₘ – A line used for control and coordination of military operations. It is usually a recognizable feature. Phase Lines are normally used to synchronize timing of operations. In this workbook, phase lines are associated with each of the five Intelligence Preparation of the Battlefield factors.

Requirement ₜₘ – These are the required skill areas needed to apply to a vacancy announcement. In other words, these are the required skills needed in order to enter into battle.

Weapon ₜₘ – Your weapon is your résumé. A tailored résumé is like a precisely calibrated weapon that will accurately hit a specific target 99% of the time.

Now that I have defined critical terms that easily associate with vacancy announcement analysis and résumé building, we will move into the next phase of your operation.

CHAPTER 3

INTELLIGENCE PREPARATION OF THE BATTLEFIELD

"CAREFULLY COMPARE THE OPPOSING ARMY WITH YOUR OWN, SO THAT YOU MAY KNOW WHERE STRENGTH IS SUPERABUNDANT AND WHERE IT IS DEFICIENT."
(SUN TZU, THE ART OF WAR)

Intelligence Preparation of the Battlefield is one of the most well recognized processes known to veterans. Veterans used Intelligence Preparation of the Battlefield when preparing for field exercises, deployments and combat. Intelligence Preparation of the Battlefield was so important that it had to be applied in order to complete the military decision making process (MDMP) and the creation of Operations Orders. This is no different from the battle you are entering. Prior to creating your résumé, you need to conduct Intelligence Preparation of the Battlefield on the vacancy announcement to which you are applying. You have to use Intelligence Preparation of the Battlefield to understand the battlefield's terrain, battlefield environment and the enemy's Avenue of Approach. In this chapter, you will learn how to use Intelligence Preparation of the Battlefield in the civilian workforce, but more immediately, how to use it for a defense contractor vacancy announcement.

The first thing you need to do is to look at yourself and your current résumé. Many individuals will spend little time on their résumé and quickly build a draft résumé, sending it to their friends for a quick review. Their friends are supportive and will most always tell them that their résumé "looks great." This is no different from a subordinate telling you that you look good in your uniform prior to leaving the base for combat…it sounds good and makes you feel good about yourself, but doesn't help you in the approaching battle. It is recommended that you proceed with calm determination and that you spend the necessary time in preparing your résumé professionally. Although your personal network of friends are extremely important and will definitely help you in obtaining a job through networking, you must ensure your résumé is tailored for a particular job in order to be competitive.

Many times individuals have already submitted the same poorly written résumé to multiple friends within their network, desperately looking for a job. However, due to the poorly written nature of their résumé, their efforts continue to meet with the same poor result. As all of you know, doing the same action repeatedly expecting a different result is the definition of insanity. Not only do they continue to submit their résumé looking for a different outcome, but now their reputation in the civilian workforce is aligned to their poorly written résumé. This lack of preparedness will inevitably be viewed and inadvertently stereotyped by the enemy as being unprepared for battle, or otherwise known as having poor work performance and unacceptable professionalism.

You must always remember that your résumé represents YOU. If your résumé is unprofessional or poorly written, it is a direct reflection of YOU. Similar to the military, your reputation is all you have in the civilian world to prove your worth. However, unlike the military, the civilian workforce normally gives you only one chance to show your worth and this normally occurs prior to being placed in a position of value.

On the other hand, in the military you can be given a job for which you are untrained and unprepared. In this particular instance, which occurs quite often in the military, you are required to demonstrate your worth no matter how difficult the task. Your reputation is based on how well you perform at positions with which you are not familiar and/or have no experience doing.

You are required to learn the details of the job quickly and the goals of your superiors immediately, while motivating and leading subordinates to perform their job at a high level. This effort ultimately will prove that you are a good worker, thereby establishing a great reputation/name for yourself. Many times this assignment will only occur for one to three years, so your energy and drive are intense for the duration. Once your tour is over, the military assesses your performance and places you in another more difficult, challenging and uncertain position requiring you to repeat the high performance your reputation has gained you.

However, unlike the military, the civilian workforce will not give you a job prior to proving yourself worthy or valuable. Therefore, since the only thing you have to show for yourself and use to initially establish a good reputation is your résumé, you must spend the necessary time building it to sufficiently resemble your professionalism, successes, worth and value to the company to which you are applying. This is especially critical since most recruiters spend only six seconds scanning résumés to determine if it is good enough to be forwarded to the hiring manager. If done properly, the civilian workforce will quickly determine your "worth" to their business and offer you an interview. If done incorrectly, you will most likely never hear back or receive feedback from the civilian workforce. Spend the time to create a powerful weapon (i.e. your résumé) and line your sight upon the Enemy/High Value Target (i.e. recruiter and/or hiring manager). In doing this you will inevitably hit the target every time and accomplish your mission.

In this workbook, you will only focus on your primary mission of obtaining an interview. Furthermore, you will not discuss the mission of obtaining the actual job, since that will be your mission during the actual interview. Only when you win each battle (vacancy announcement battle and the interview battle) will you actually win the war and be hired for the job.

What is the Intelligence Preparation of the Battlefield? Intelligence Preparation of the Battlefield is a systematic, continuous process of analyzing the enemy, the area of operation and the battlefield. It is also a process to analyze the civilian workforce environment in a specific location and/or job skill.

Intelligence Preparation of the Battlefield is designed to support applicant analysis, job analysis and your decision making process. Applying the Intelligence Preparation of the Battlefield process to defense contractor vacancy announcements and résumés will help you apply and maximize your competitiveness at critical points during the review process by ensuring you meet each battlefield objective. Only when you have successfully accomplished each objective, sequentially, can you align the site of your weapon, aim your weapon upon the enemy/High Value Target and hit the target to take control of the key terrain.

To start, think about the following areas throughout this workbook:

1. Determine "The Enemy's" method of writing the vacancy.
2. Determine "The Enemy's" résumé review process.
3. Determine the type of vacancy announcement.
4. Determine vacancy announcement requirements.

Intelligence Preparation of the Battlefield for defense contractor vacancy announcements and résumés is a continuous process which consists of five steps, which you perform each time you conduct Intelligence Preparation of the Battlefield. Think of these as Phase Lines on a battlefield, each bringing you closer to mission accomplishment:

1. Phase Line (Describe)   – Write a long résumé.

2. Phase Line (Analyze) – Analyze the announcement.
3. Phase Line (Evaluate) – Evaluate similar VAs.
4. Phase Line (Target) – Tailor/Target a Résumé.
5. Mission Accomplished – Get the Interview.

As you can see from the map above, this will be your battlefield that you must use throughout this workbook. The green start button on the bottom left is where you are right now. The green arrow is your Avenue of Approach. As shown on the following map, you will "mentally" take a walk to each objective, sequentially, in order to move to the next phase of the operation. In the following picture, your route is shown via the dotted black line, moving from the start position to objective one. Once you complete an objective, you can then move to the next objective. There are three objectives per phase and there are four phase lines. Once you have completed all nine objectives, you will move into the targeting phase where you will calibrate your weapon and fire upon the enemy to gain the key terrain.

The Intelligence Preparation of the Battlefield process is continuous. You conduct Intelligence Preparation of the Battlefield prior to developing an Operations Order for battle, now you need to use Intelligence Preparation of the Battlefield prior to writing your targeted résumé and definitely prior to applying to a vacancy. You must ensure you synchronize your résumé with your Intelligence Preparation of the Battlefield of the vacancy announcement, similar to developing different Operations Orders for different military missions. You also must continue to perform Intelligence Preparation of the Battlefield for each vacancy announcement. Each function in the process is performed continuously to ensure that—

1. Your IPB analysis remains complete and valid.
2. Your AA and strategy are defined throughout your résumé.
3. You properly prepare for an updated version of your résumé.

OPERATION: CIVILIAN RÉSUMÉ

WARNING ORDER
MESSAGE

Your mission is to take control of the key terrain and obtain the interview. Now that I have given you the Warning Order for your mission and officially notified you that a battle is about to begin, your encounter with the enemy is inevitable. It is now up to you, and only you, to accomplish your mission.

Good Luck,
BB

CHAPTER 4

PHASE LINE – DESCRIBE

Write a Long Résumé

"The good fighters of old first put themselves beyond the possibility of defeat, and then waited for an opportunity of defeating the enemy."
(Sun Tzu, The Art of War)

In starting your mission, you must develop Phase Lines (PL) in order to achieve progressively small successes and milestones, which will ultimately culminate in successfully targeting the High Value Target and acquiring your key terrain. Within each Phase Line, you must accomplish three objectives before moving to the next Phase Line. Ultimately, once you accomplish each throughout each phase of the operation, you will have successfully accomplished your mission. Similar to a battlefield, you must ensure your route is flexible and maneuvers through the terrain, accomplishing each objective in order to succeed.

Let's take a look at this phase of our operation. Here you have three objectives that you must accomplish in order to move to the next phase.

Objective 1 – List all of your work assignments/positions.
Objective 2 – Describe your duties, responsibilities and impacts.
Objective 3 – Quantify all activities within each assignment.

The DESCRIBE phase is one of the most important phases when transitioning from one job to another, especially for fellow veterans. Properly describing your past experience is a critical element of your military transition and one that most veterans have never spent the necessary time to finish. Therefore, if you are the one who takes my advice and writes a long résumé, you will have more of an advantage in applying to multiple vacancies than the majority of your competition.

OPERATION: CIVILIAN RÉSUMÉ

What is meant by a long résumé? A long résumé is a résumé that contains all of your work assignments and a thorough description of everything you did within each work assignment. During the Describe phase, you will learn how to identify the details needed for a long résumé. All of us have had numerous job positions and numerous job titles. Most people have spent one to three years in their position, unlike your civilian counterparts who may have spent 10 to 15 years in a specific job. This initially causes you some consternation and potentially makes you less qualified than your civilian counterparts. However, if you spend the necessary time to develop and expand your duties, responsibilities and successes and/or impacts for

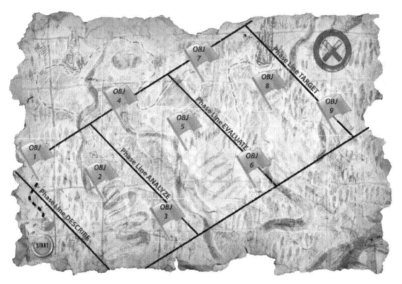

each of your work history assignments, your depth of experience and degree of expertise will become more competitive than your civilian counterparts.

Let's get started....

OBJECTIVE 1

Job Titles. The first thing that you need to do is to list all of the job titles that you have ever held. This means <u>literally all</u> of the job titles and job positions that you have held throughout your military and civilian career. This may seem like a daunting task, however, it is definitely necessary. Each job description should be approximately one page long. However, at this point in the process you don't have to worry about the length of your long résumé. Just remember, that in a defense contracting job, your salary is normally based on years of experience related to the job to which you are applying. Therefore, unlike the private sector résumé, a defense contracting résumé can have over 20 years of experience within it. As an example, a typical résumé for a retired military officer or senior non-commissioned officer with a lengthy career in the same general career field, will span a 20 to 30 year career. Therefore, the résumé for this particular person will be up to four pages in length. You may think that this sounds like it may be too long, but when your salary is tied to your years of experience, you definitely need to ensure that your years of experience are clearly conveyed in your résumé.

> <u>CAUTION:</u> One bit of caution, however, do not submit your long résumé to vacancy announcements. You should only use your long résumé as a tool to extract information required when tailoring and targeting your résumé to a vacancy announcement. You should not use your long résumé to apply to jobs. Why is this? Because your long résumé has no strategy attached to it; it has no theme development, you have **not tailored** it to a specific vacancy announcement, is **not targeted** to a specific vacancy

announcement and is only written as your autobiography, which is unacceptable when applying to a defense contractor position.

Dates. After writing out your job titles and work history, place the month and year that you held each position to the right of the page. For instance, if you were a mechanic from April 2001 to April 2002, then that's what you would put on your long résumé. In addition, on your long résumé you need to place the location in which you worked underneath each job title as well as the duty assignment and unit or organization in which you worked, as shown below:

> Mechanic   Apr 01 – Apr 02
> 82d Airborne Division
> Fort Bragg, NC

OBJECTIVE 2

Duties and Responsibilities. Throughout your work history, and underneath each position title, you need to list the details of your duties and responsibilities. Most importantly, you must explain/describe the impact that you had in each assignment and/or the positive outcome of your activities. In these descriptive statements, it is recommended that you write them in a narrative format to ensure your list is complete. Describe all of your experiences, such as the forms that you used, the regulations and policy numbers that you referenced, as well as any computer programs, databases or equipment that you utilized. Please understand that in a long résumé you need to expand your descriptions and use lots of detail.

Awards. Many veterans place their awards at the end of their résumé. It is recommended however, to refrain from placing your awards in your résumé at all, but rather place the reason for the award in your résumé as a positive impact or accomplishment. To clarify, if you look at each of your awards, such as the Army Achievement Medal, Meritorious Service Medal, etc. most service members have received these same awards, therefore making your résumé no different from other Soldiers/applicants. However, when focusing on the reason why you received the awards or the reason why your supervisor submitted you for the award, your résumé then transcends to something completely different from everyone else. Therefore, you need to list the reasons why you received the award(s) within the appropriate and respective work history assignment to demonstrate how you successfully accomplished your duties and responsibilities.

Training. Make sure to list all training courses that you attended and from which school you graduated. Also, make sure to list the associated location and the year completed or graduated. Please see the below as an example:

| BNCOC (97B) | Fort Huachuca, AZ | 1993 |

Certification. Make sure to list all qualifications and certifications in this area, the location and/or organization from which you received certification and year received. Examples of certifications would be Project Management Professional (PMP), Certified Information Systems Security Professional (CISSP), Certified Fraud Examiner (CFE), etc.

Additional skills. In this section, you should place all of the skills that do not fit nicely under each of the above titles. For example, you should list your proficiency level in this section for the following: foreign languages, Microsoft Office, Microsoft Word, Microsoft PowerPoint, Microsoft Excel, Microsoft Access and Microsoft Project etc.

OBJECTIVE 3

Quantify your work history. In this section, you need to look back into each work assignment duty description and quantify all of your activities. Look at your roles and responsibilities, your duties and accomplishments and try to quantify everything. When stating that you were in charge of people, make sure to list how many people for whom you were responsible and their job specialties. Take enough time to list the number and types of reports for which you were responsible to manage. You should use this same concept for everything that you did, whether it was with money, tools, buildings, reports, etc… you must quantify, quantify, quantify. Why is this so important? This is critical to a good résumé because most other applicants do not spend the necessary time to quantify their activities. Therefore, when the hiring manager reads the un-quantified résumé, he/she will interpret it as having generic statements of duties and responsibilities with no substance. On the other hand, if you quantify everything in your résumé you will convey that you have the depth and breadth of experience that meets the vacancy announcement requirements and exceeds other applicants.

OPERATION: CIVILIAN RÉSUMÉ

WARNING ORDER
MESSAGE

Congratulations! You have successfully accomplished all three objectives within Phase Line DESCRIBE. You are now prepared to cross into Phase Line ANALYZE. As you move forward, do not be complacent. Phase Line ANALYZE will test your mental acuity in analyzing the enemy's intent on the battlefield.

Good Luck,
BB

CHAPTER 5

PHASE LINE – ANALYZE

Analyze the Battlefield

> "THE ART OF WAR, THEN, IS GOVERNED BY FIVE CONSTANT FACTORS, TO BE TAKEN INTO ACCOUNT IN ONE'S DELIBERATIONS, WHEN SEEKING TO DETERMINE THE CONDITIONS OBTAINING IN THE FIELD. THESE ARE: (1) THE MORAL LAW; (2) HEAVEN; (3) EARTH; (4) THE COMMANDER; (5) METHOD AND DISCIPLINE."
> (SUN TZU, THE ART OF WAR)

In Phase Line Analyze of the Intelligence Preparation of the Battlefield process, you will be analyzing the battlefield (the vacancy announcement). In this chapter, you will learn how to analyze vacancy requirements, job descriptions and how to identify key words within the vacancy announcement. You will focus your efforts on the "Junior Declassification Analyst" position in order to understand the concepts and principles in which to apply to all other vacancy announcements. In order to move to the next phase, you will need to accomplish each objective below successfully —

Objective 4 - Analyze the Mandatory Requirements.
Objective 5 - Analyze the Job Description.
Objective 6 - Identify the key words.

As you move through the battlefield of vacancy announcement analysis, you need to focus your attention on the upcoming objective. In Objective 4, you need to identify the mandatory requirements of the vacancy announcement, which requires an in-depth evaluation and assessment. Identify and analyze the job description, roles and responsibilities, required skills, required experience, required education, required security clearance and any additional requirements specific to the vacancy announcement. Generally, these are analyzed in-depth and are the main focus of a tailored résumé.

OPERATION: CIVILIAN RÉSUMÉ

You must focus your analytical efforts on the areas of significance to your experience. You need to base your analysis on the requirements of the vacancy announcement and not what you think or have been told the requirements are. Focusing on the vacancy announcement, itself, without any distracters, will not only influence your operation by tailoring your weapon appropriately, but will immediately convey to the enemy/hiring manager that you are qualified for the job and need to be interviewed immediately.

Defining significant requirements of the vacancy announcement will aid in identifying gaps in your current work history. You must identify gaps in your résumé to ensure your résumé focuses on the hiring manager's requirements and desires. Once you finish your analysis, the specific key words and work requirements for the job vacancy become your targeted focus.

Now, take a few minutes to focus on these critical objectives and start calibrating your weapon/résumé.

OBJECTIVE 4

Mandatory Requirements – To accomplish this objective, you need to identify the mandatory requirements of the job vacancy by highlighting all key words within the mandatory requirements section. Make sure you use multiple colors and underlining techniques for your keyword identification. One process that you can use is to highlight the words in yellow highlighter and red text, and sometimes underlining. However, this is completely up to you, but try to remain as consistent as possible with each vacancy announcement that you analyze and evaluate. Again, focus only on the mandatory requirements of the following vacancy announcement.

Junior Declassification Analyst - Job ID: 85252BR

Job Description:

Conduct initial declassification reviews in support of the Department of the Navy (DoN) Automatic Declassification Program. The Junior Declassification Analyst will use their analytical skills to apply DoN policy and procedures in making determinations on documents for declassification, exemption, exclusion or referral to other agencies. Each candidate must have demonstrated strong analytical skills, reading comprehension, attention to detail, and organizational abilities.

Required:

Final DoD Top Secret clearance or the ability to obtain one.
Bachelor's degree in History, Political Science, or International Affairs or three years relevant work experience required. Successfully passing DoN initial declassification training and the Department of Energy's Historical Records Restricted Data Reviewers Course.

Document Review:

Analyze unclassified and classified documents to determine the appropriate action needed in accordance with section 3.3 of Executive Order (E.O.) 13526. Proper understanding of document markings and ultimately proper handling. Working knowledge of exemption categories 1-9 under section 3.3 of E.O. 13526. Ability to properly recognize actual and possible nuclear weapons and intelligence information in all types of documents. Ability to correctly apply the DoN Declassification Guide. Able to research information and ask questions to make informed decisions. Ability to apply proper records management techniques to ensure the integrity of reviewed material. Assist in any other role or function that supports the efforts of the project. Ability to move boxes weighing between 15 to 25 pounds.

Employment Type	Full-Time
Education	4 Year Degree
Experience	At least 3 year(s)
Manages Others	Not Specified

NOTES:

_____

_____

_____

_____

_____

_____

_____

_____

Objective 4 – Answer: In this example on the next page, you can see the highlighted words in red and yellow. The key words in this section identify the clearance requirement, the word "or," and the "ability to obtain." Additionally, a bachelor's degree is required in history, political science or international affairs. However, this requirement also accepts three years of relevant work experience instead of the education requirement. Additionally, once hired, you have to pass a Department of the Navy course in declassification training successfully and the Department of Energy's historical records restricted data reviewers course successfully. Therefore, it is necessary to add any declassification training that you have to your résumé.

OPERATION: CIVILIAN RÉSUMÉ

Junior Declassification Analyst - Job ID: 85252BR
Job Description:
Conduct initial declassification reviews in support of the Department of the Navy (DoN) Automatic Declassification Program. The Junior Declassification Analyst will use their analytical skills to apply DoN policy and procedures in making determinations on documents for declassification, exemption, exclusion or referral to other agencies. Each candidate must have demonstrated strong analytical skills, reading comprehension, attention to detail, and organizational abilities.
Required:
Final DoD Top Secret security clearance or the ability to obtain one. Bachelor's degree in History, Political Science, or International Affairs or three years relevant work experience required. Successfully passing DoN initial declassification training and the Department of Energy's Historical Records Restricted Data Reviewers Course.
Document Review:
Analyze unclassified and classified documents to determine the appropriate action needed in accordance with section 3.3 of Executive Order (E.O.) 13526. Proper understanding of document markings and ultimately proper handling. Working knowledge of exemption categories 1-9 under section 3.3 of E.O. 13526. Ability to properly recognize actual and possible nuclear weapons and intelligence information in all types of documents. Ability to correctly apply the DoN Declassification Guide. Able to research information and ask questions to make informed decisions. Ability to apply proper records management techniques to ensure the integrity of reviewed material. Assist in any other role or function that supports the efforts of the project. Ability to move boxes weighing between 15 to 25 pounds.

Employment Type	Full-Time
Education	4 Year Degree
Experience	At least 3 year(s)
Manages Others	Not Specified

OBJECTIVE 5

Job Description – Now you must analyze the Job Description in the following vacancy announcement by highlighting key terms, patterns and what you feel the hiring manager wants to see in an applicant.

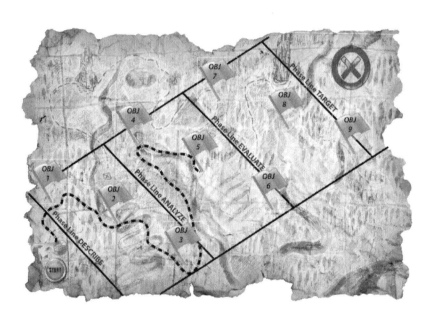

Junior Declassification Analyst - Job ID: 85252BR
Job Description:
Conduct initial declassification reviews in support of the Department of the Navy (DoN) Automatic Declassification Program. The Junior Declassification Analyst will use their analytical skills to apply DoN policy and procedures in making determinations on documents for declassification, exemption, exclusion or referral to other agencies. Each candidate must have demonstrated strong analytical skills, reading comprehension, attention to detail, and organizational abilities.
Required:
Final DoD Top Secret security clearance or the ability to obtain one. Bachelor's degree in History, Political Science, or International Affairs or three years relevant work experience required. Successfully passing DoN initial declassification training and the Department of Energy's Historical Records Restricted Data Reviewers Course.
Document Review:
Analyze unclassified and classified documents to determine the appropriate action needed in accordance with section 3.3 of Executive Order (E.O.) 13526. Proper understanding of document markings and ultimately proper handling. Working knowledge of exemption categories 1-9 under section 3.3 of E.O. 13526. Ability to properly recognize actual and possible nuclear weapons and intelligence information in all types of documents. Ability to correctly apply the DoN Declassification Guide. Able to research information and ask questions to make informed decisions. Ability to apply proper records management techniques to ensure the integrity of reviewed material. Assist in any other role or function that supports the efforts of the project. Ability to move boxes weighing between 15 to 25 pounds.

Employment Type	Full-Time
Education	4 Year Degree
Experience	At least 3 year(s)
Manages Others	Not Specified

NOTES:

_____

_____

_____

_____

_____

_____

_____

Objective 5 – Answer: As you can see in the following example, the highlighted key words are in yellow and red text. The word "conduct" is extremely important and alludes to the fact that the hiring manager would like the applicant to describe how they have actually conducted declassification reviews. Also, the word "Navy" is highlighted because if you have worked for the Navy you will also have more of an advantage over other applicants. Also highlighted is the word "declassification program," and, later on in the paragraph, "declassification exemptions exclusion."

One key element with these highlights is that the word declassification is repeated multiple times. Although you can make the assumption that it's repeated multiple times because the job title is for a declassification analyst, the applicant who targets their résumé for this position should interpret the repetitive nature of this word as extremely important and necessary to utilize within their résumé. Additionally, highlighted in red text "analytical skills," "making determinations," "demonstrated strong analytical skills," "reading comprehension," "attention to detail," and "organizational abilities." All of these are capabilities that the applicant must demonstrate throughout their résumé. By demonstrate, it is implied that the reader of your résumé must interpret what you have written as being capable of conducting these key words.

Junior Declassification Analyst - Job ID: 85252BR

Job Description:
Conduct initial declassification reviews in support of the Department of the Navy (DoN) Automatic Declassification Program. The Junior Declassification Analyst will use their analytical skills to apply DoN policy and procedures in making determinations on documents for declassification, exemption, exclusion or referral to other agencies. Each candidate must have demonstrated strong analytical skills, reading comprehension, attention to detail, and organizational abilities.

Required:
Final DoD Top Secret security clearance or the ability to obtain one. Bachelor's degree in History, Political Science, or International Affairs or three years relevant work experience required. Successfully passing DoN initial declassification training and the Department of Energy's Historical Records Restricted Data Reviewers Course.

Document Review:
Analyze unclassified and classified documents to determine the appropriate action needed in accordance with section 3.3 of Executive Order (E.O.) 13526. Proper understanding of document markings and ultimately proper handling. Working knowledge of exemption categories 1-9 under section 3.3 of E.O. 13526. Ability to properly recognize actual and possible nuclear weapons and intelligence information in all types of documents. Ability to correctly apply the DoN Declassification Guide. Able to research information and ask questions to make informed decisions. Ability to apply proper records management techniques to ensure the integrity of reviewed material. Assist in any other role or function that supports the efforts of the project. Ability to move boxes weighing between 15 to 25 pounds.

Employment Type	Full-Time
Education	4 Year Degree
Experience	At least 3 year(s)
Manages Others	Not Specified

OBJECTIVE 6

Analyze the rest of the vacancy announcement – Now you need to identify the key words throughout the rest of the job vacancy announcement.

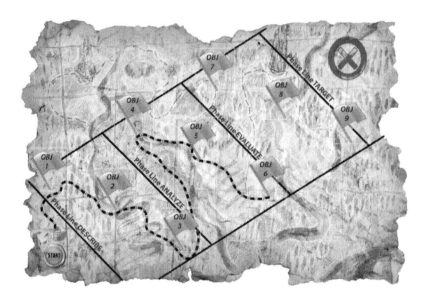

OPERATION: CIVILIAN RÉSUMÉ

Junior Declassification Analyst - Job ID: 85252BR

Job Description:
Conduct initial declassification reviews in support of the Department of the Navy (DoN) Automatic Declassification Program. The Junior Declassification Analyst will use their analytical skills to apply DoN policy and procedures in making determinations on documents for declassification, exemption, exclusion or referral to other agencies. Each candidate must have demonstrated strong analytical skills, reading comprehension, attention to detail, and organizational abilities.

Required:
Final DoD Top Secret security clearance or the ability to obtain one. Bachelor's degree in History, Political Science, or International Affairs or three years relevant work experience required. Successfully passing DoN initial declassification training and the Department of Energy's Historical Records Restricted Data Reviewers Course.

Document Review:
Analyze unclassified and classified documents to determine the appropriate action needed in accordance with section 3.3 of Executive Order (E.O.) 13526. Proper understanding of document markings and ultimately proper handling. Working knowledge of exemption categories 1-9 under section 3.3 of E.O. 13526. Ability to properly recognize actual and possible nuclear weapons and intelligence information in all types of documents. Ability to correctly apply the DoN Declassification Guide. Able to research information and ask questions to make informed decisions. Ability to apply proper records management techniques to ensure the integrity of reviewed material. Assist in any other role or function that supports the efforts of the project. Ability to move boxes weighing between 15 to 25 pounds.

Employment Type	Full-Time
Education	4 Year Degree
Experience	At least 3 year(s)
Manages Others	Not Specified

NOTES:

_____
_____
_____
_____
_____
_____
_____
_____
_____

Objective 6 – Answer: When analyzing key words in the rest of the vacancy announcement, make sure you identify those key words that you believe the hiring manager would like to see in your résumé. Highlighted is the word "*analyze*" to ensure that when tailoring a résumé for this vacancy the word analyze is utilized within the bulletized duties and responsibilities. Next, you need to include the words "*unclassified and classified*" within your work history. You should also include these throughout multiple positions that you have held. Although most military professionals normally assume working with unclassified and classified material is a fact that does not need to be placed in their résumé, especially if you have a security clearance, the fact that it's listed in the vacancy announcement requires that you place it in your résumé. Highlighted in red is a key element within this job vacancy: "*Section 3.3 of Executive Order EO 13526*." This is important because not only is it listed multiple times, but also it is a direct reference to which the vacancy refers. Therefore, if you have not worked directly with this referenced document, you should look at "*Section 3.3 of Executive Order EO 13526*" online, read the document thoroughly and be prepared to list it in your résumé and/or answer questions during the interview about it.

Further down, the vacancy states "*document markings*" and "*proper handling*," which are again assumed tasks that everyone with a security clearance conducts. However, since the hiring manager lists these terms within the vacancy announcement, you must ensure you list the same words within your résumé. Do not take anything for granted and assume the reader accurately interprets what you are trying to convey.

One key element that seems to be buried within this job vacancy is the requirement to have "*recognized actual or possible nuclear weapons*." This statement is slightly confusing since the overall narrative of this vacancy announcement is so generic. However, since this statement is so unnatural within this vacancy description, it conveys that it is a critical element and qualifier of this position for which the hiring manager is looking. The following words that are highlighted in red, such as apply (which is written twice), research and ask questions, are key action verbs that you must include in your résumé as well.

Tip 1: Pay particular attention to verbs that are mentioned more than once. This is a key indicator of verbs that the hiring manager likes to see in résumés.

Tip 2: When documents are listed within a vacancy announcement, make sure to search them on the internet and become familiar with the documents. Try to discern how your work experience translates into the language of that particular reference.

Junior Declassification Analyst - Job ID: 85252BR

Job Description:
Conduct initial declassification reviews in support of the Department of the Navy (DoN) Automatic Declassification Program. The Junior Declassification Analyst will use their analytical skills to apply DoN policy and procedures in making determinations on documents for declassification, exemption, exclusion or referral to other agencies. Each candidate must have demonstrated strong analytical skills, reading comprehension, attention to detail, and organizational abilities.

Required:
Final DoD Top Secret security clearance or the ability to obtain one. Bachelor's degree in History, Political Science, or International Affairs or three years relevant work experience required. Successfully passing DoN initial declassification training and the Department of Energy's Historical Records Restricted Data Reviewers Course.

Document Review:
Analyze unclassified and classified documents to determine the appropriate action needed in accordance with section 3.3 of Executive Order (E.O.) 13526. Proper understanding of document markings and ultimately proper handling. Working knowledge of exemption categories 1-9 under section 3.3 of E.O. 13526. Ability to properly recognize actual and possible nuclear weapons and intelligence information in all types of documents. Ability to correctly apply the DoN Declassification Guide. Able to research information and ask questions to make informed decisions. Ability to apply proper records management techniques to ensure the integrity of reviewed material. Assist in any other role or function that supports the efforts of the project. Ability to move boxes weighing between 15 to 25 pounds.

Employment Type	Full-Time
Job Type	Other
Education	4 Year Degree
Experience	At least 3 year(s)
Manages Others	Not Specified

Tip 3: Be cautious if you see terms, procedures and processes, and/or the term cycle within a vacancy announcement, such as Project Management Professional (PMP). Search these terms on the internet to identify the specific lexicon used within each. These terms are used throughout vacancy announcements in order to describe multiple key words at once. Therefore, you need to research these terms as it relates to the vacancy announcement in order to identify the key words associated with them. Once you identify the key words, try to associate your work experience with these words and use these words to describe your expertise.

```
          WARNING ORDER
             MESSAGE

Congratulations! You have successfully
accomplished all six objectives within
Phase Line DESCRIBE and Phase Line
ANALYZE. You are now prepared to cross
into Phase Line EVALUATE. As you move
forward, do not rush through the
process. Phase Line EVALUATE will test
your stamina in evaluating multiple
vacancy announcements.

Good Luck,
BB
```

CHAPTER 6

PHASE LINE – EVALUATE

Evaluate Your Area of Operation

"KNOWLEDGE OF THE ENEMY'S DISPOSITIONS CAN ONLY BE OBTAINED FROM OTHER MEN."
(SUN TZU, THE ART OF WAR)

In this phase of the Intelligence Preparation of the Battlefield process, you will be required to obtain multiple vacancy announcements for the same type of job vacancy. The key is to place each vacancy announcement next to each other, analyze each individual vacancy announcement and then analyze each of the vacancy announcements against each other. This effort, although tedious, will pay off in dividends when tailoring your résumé. In order to make it through this phase, you need to accomplish each of the below objectives successfully —

Objective 7 – Evaluate multiple job *requirements* for similar vacancy announcements.
Objective 8 – Evaluate multiple job *descriptions* for similar vacancy announcements.
Objective 9 – Evaluate *key words* from similar vacancy announcements.

OBJECTIVE 7

Evaluate Multiple Job Requirements. To ensure that you target your résumé appropriately, you will need to analyze and evaluate three to five other vacancy announcements of similar types. When analyzing these other vacancies, you will need to analyze the job requirements again, the job descriptions again and all the key words again by highlighting and underlining and even color-coding as much as possible. In short, you will need to perform the objectives in Phase Line-Analyze for three to five vacancy announcements.

When conducted appropriately, this activity propels your résumé quickly into another Phase Line and elevates your experience to a "Subject Matter Expert" (also known as a "SME"). Your résumé will take on a tailored approach in order to target vacancies directly.

This is one major aspect of résumé writing that most transitioning Soldiers and veterans fail to do. Many veterans say that they have applied to hundreds of positions, yet never receive a reply from the hiring manager or recruiter. When asked what's wrong with their résumé, the first question asked is "Are you using the same résumé for all of the positions to which you are applying?" 99% of the time the answer is yes. To ensure this does not happen to you, carefully and skillfully achieve each objective in this workbook.

To better understand the way forward and to better understand the way you need to process information when writing résumés, you have to take a step back and recall your military doctrine. Military doctrine, such as Intelligence Preparation of the Battlefield, is what veterans have spent many hours conducting prior to field exercises, deployments and combat missions. Remember the many hours you spent conducting research on your enemy, identifying all key enemy locations, identifying all possible enemy Courses of Action and creating your own friendly force Courses of Action as well. As you recall all of the "rock drills" (miniature sized versions of a battlefield) and the preparation and briefings conducted by the S3/Operations Officer and Battle Captains from the Battalion to the Brigade to the Division and Corps prior to any and all operational activity. All of this preparation was conducted after receipt of the Warning Order and prior to Operations Order development. This effort, although exhausting, was required to ensure the Operations Order was appropriate for the upcoming mission.

Your transition out of the military into the civilian world is no different. As well, for those veterans already in the civilian workforce, your preparation from one position into another is just as difficult today due to economical issues like sequestration, budget cuts and the transition out of Iraq and Afghanistan. Jobs are less frequently announced and have hundreds of applicants applying to the same position. However, the major problem seen with veterans is that they fail to properly prepare for the transition, ultimately having the same effect as if they failed to prepare for battle. So in order to help you prepare for this transition you must strategically walk through the battlefield carefully and methodically in order to achieve each objective. Only then will you accomplish your mission. This methodology will prepare you to move into a second career and/or a defense contractor position.

OPERATION: CIVILIAN RÉSUMÉ

OBJECTIVE 8

Evaluate Multiple Job Requirements. The time that it takes to analyze multiple vacancy announcements will pay-off three-fold in the end. Do not sell yourself short and start sending out a non-tailored, non-targeted résumé, hoping that you will get a job. You must spend the necessary time to prepare as you did in the military. You must analyze all aspects of your enemy. Therefore, you need to analyze all types of job vacancies to which you want to apply. For instance, in this example, this vacancy is for a

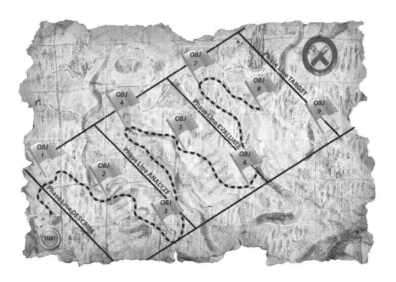

declassification analyst. Therefore, you need to search online and obtain multiple declassification analyst job vacancy announcements. When you have three to five job vacancy announcements for a declassification analyst, you need to analyze each one very closely. You need to go back to Phase Line Analyze and make sure you have highlighted all the key skills and all the key words within the job descriptions and requirements. No different from your military service, you will eventually see a pattern used by the enemy/hiring manager when writing these vacancies.

Why is there a pattern? Most likely, there is a pattern because the hiring manager extracted the job descriptions, the job requirements and any additional information directly from a government contract. Therefore, each higher-level position will be described differently, based on the government requirements. The government must distinctly categorize each level of subject matter expertise so the defense contractor clearly understands the salary range for each qualified applicant. If you identify the critical terms used between different levels of experience (i.e. novice, junior, senior or level I, II or III) for a declassification analyst, you may very well find yourself in a higher salary level based on your experience compared to the contract requirements. You must use this pattern to your advantage within your résumé, therefore making it a tailored résumé that you have targeted to the particular job vacancy announcement.

OBJECTIVE 9

Key Words. Phase Line Analyze identifies the effects of key words from the applicant's perspective as well as the hiring manager's perspective. Additionally, to exploit your enemy's tendency to identify areas in your

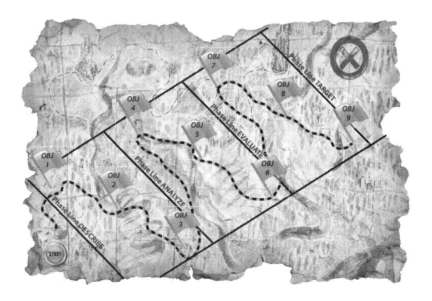

résumé that do not make you qualified, you must further identify the competencies that support the requirements and key words. Only then can you turn work history that initially appears unrelated into work history that supports the vacancy announcement requirements. For a list of basic competencies, please refer to Appendix D.

Many military personnel place non-relevant work history into their résumé, attempting to fill gaps in time. Furthermore, other transitioning members arbitrarily leave out non-relevant work experience to the vacancy announcement without attempting to identify vacancy announcement competencies that they may be able to support by using this apparent "non-related" work. However, both methods are potentially dangerous and run a risk of causing you not to be selected for an interview.

When tailoring and targeting your résumé to a vacancy announcement, you must ensure that all work history is relevant to the vacancy announcement. However, this is not as easy as it sounds and does not mean for you to remove work history that you <u>can</u> tailor to the vacancy announcement. If you have work history that does not support the vacancy announcement directly, look further into the vacancy announcement requirements and further analyze your work history to identify the supporting competencies to the vacancy announcement.

More times than not, you will be able to tailor your "non-relevant" work history a certain way to ensure that it is relevant to the vacancy announcement. The way to do this is to identify the competencies of the vacancy announcement and modify your work history job titles, responsibilities and accomplishments to support these competencies. Therefore, in doing this you have now just changed your "non-relevant" work history into relevant work history. You can now start to tailor aspects of your work history, which initially appear to have no relevancy to the vacancy announcement, into related work history.

OPERATIONS ORDER
MESSAGE

Congratulations! You have successfully accomplished all nine objectives within Phase Line DESCRIBE, ANALYZE and EVALUATE. You are now ready to cross into the final phase: Phase Line TARGET. As you move forward, make sure to carefully calibrate your weapon, tailor your résumé and accurately aim at the target so you can hit the target and successfully accomplish your mission. You are almost there…

Good Luck,
BB

CHAPTER 7

PHASE LINE – TARGET

Write a Tailored and Targeted Résumé

"Standing on the defensive indicates insufficient strength; attacking, a superabundance of strength."
(Sun Tzu, The Art of War)

In Phase Line Target of the Intelligence Preparation of the Battlefield process, you will learn how to target your résumé to a specific vacancy announcement. This is the last phase of the process and the most critical. Your efforts up to this point have prepared you for the upcoming objectives. Now you must use all that you have learned in order to target the enemy/High Value Target (hiring manager) accurately and gain the key terrain (the interview). Think of this phase as steadying your weapon in order to shoot the target precisely. In this case, you must methodically prepare your weapon/résumé, accurately aim your weapon/résumé to the target and accurately fire your weapon/résumé solidifying that you have tailored and targeted your résumé to the vacancy announcement requirements. To progress through this phase, you must accomplish each of the following objectives—

Objective Ready – Choose a résumé format.
Objective Aim – Tailor your résumé to the announcement.
Objective Fire – Target your résumé to the announcement.

OBJECTIVE READY

Choose a Résumé Format. When choosing a résumé format, you need to be especially cognizant of what type of résumé and/or cover letter the enemy/hiring manager would like to see. Obviously, when reading the vacancy announcement, you should have a good idea as to how you are going to place all the key words together and throughout your résumé so that your résumé reads quickly and fluidly. Hiring managers and recruiters normally spend between six and ten seconds scanning and reviewing a résumé. Because they have hundreds of résumés to review, they must quickly scan each résumé to determine whether it is worthy of their time to read. Therefore, the résumé shown in this chapter is one that I feel works extremely well when targeting a vacancy announcement and will help you in identifying where your résumé needs calibrated.

Bruce Benedict, PMP
(MAJ/O-4, US Army, Retired)

Address
Address
(XXX) 207-2716
Bruce@BattlefieldResumes.com

HIGHLIGHTS OF QUALIFICATIONS
TOP SECRET/SCI (2009), BA in HISTORY
Skilled **Declassification Analyst** *with experience and proficiency in the following:*

- Classification/Declassification Guides
- Exemption Cat. 1-9, Sec 3.3, EO13526
- Classified Document Marking Procedures
- Unclassified & Classified Document Analysis
- Nuclear Weapon Identification

PROFESSIONAL EXPERIENCE

Intelligence Analyst (MAJ)　　　　　　　　　　　**Aug 12 – Present**
Unit and Location

- Oversees the proper marking of over 500 classified documents to ensure compliance with exemption categories 1-9 of section 3.3, EO 13526.
- Identifies possible Nuclear Weapon delivery systems and other intelligence information, such as captured weapons, arms trafficking activities focused on the Middle East, Africa and the EUCOM AOR.
- Initiates hundreds of classified Source Directed Requirements and over 50 collection emphasis messages to ensure questions to collection assets are appropriately written to ensure Intelligence Gaps are answered.
- Warns Intelligence Community of destabilization activities.
- Final reviewer of analysis and synchronizes MS PowerPoint presentations, which includes eight Commands and up to 40 personnel.

EDUCATION

MA in Military History	School, Location (100 credit hours)(exp grad)	2016
BA in History	School, Location	1988
AA in Liberal Arts	School, Location	1985

TRAINING

MI Officer Basic Course	School, Location	2010
Intelligence in Combating Terrorism Course	School, Location	2010
Officer Candidate School	School, Location	2009
Small Group Instruction Course	School, Location	2009
Basic Instructor Training Course	School, Location	2008
Battle Staff Course	School, Location	2007
Safety Officer Course	School, Location	2006

OPERATION: CIVILIAN RÉSUMÉ

OBJECTIVE AIM

Tailor Your Résumé . To tailor your résumé to the vacancy announcement, you must ensure that you list all of your relevant work experience with a month and year format. Listing your work history this way will ensure that the hiring manager and recruiter can accurately calculate how many years of experience, collectively, you have in

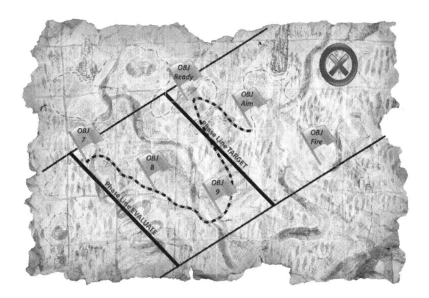

relationship to the vacancy announcement. You must do this critical step correctly. The identification of your years of relevant experience is critical because in defense contracting your salary is normally based on years of experience as listed in the government contract to which the contracting company is trying to fill.

Additionally, you need to build a theme throughout your résumé to ensure that each of your job titles correctly identifies your activities within each work history assignment, yet are tailored to the vacancy itself. In other words, if you need to modify each job title to more accurately convey what you did in that particular job, then do it. At the same time, your modified job title should support an aspect of the vacancy announcement. You must list the organization or unit that you were part of and the location in which you served.

The first and second bullet of each work history must directly support the first half of the first page of your targeted résumé, therefore, directly supporting the vacancy announcement. In other words, you must look at the top half portion of your résumé as the index to a book. The job titles can be associated with chapters in the book. The bulletized impact statements within each work history assignment can be associated with the narrative within each chapter of your book. Collectively, all of the information supports the index to your book and therefore ultimately supports the vacancy announcement. If you do this correctly, whomever reads your résumé will peruse it quickly and immediately identify that you are highly qualified for the position and deserve an interview. Please see the following résumé as an example of the above description. Notice how all of the dates are aligned to the right for easy viewing and how the job titles are aligned to the left, above the unit and location.

OPERATION: CIVILIAN RÉSUMÉ

Bruce Benedict, PMP
(MAJ/O-4, US Army, Retired)

Address (XXX) 207-2716
Address Bruce@BattlefieldRésumés.com

HIGHLIGHTS OF QUALIFICATIONS
TOP SECRET/SCI (2009), BA in HISTORY
Skilled **Declassification Analyst** *with experience and proficiency in the following:*

- Classification/Declassification Guides
- Exemption Cat. 1-9, Sec 3.3, EO13526
- Classified Document Marking Procedures
- Unclassified & Classified Document Analysis
- Nuclear Weapon Identification

PROFESSIONAL EXPERIENCE

Intelligence Analyst (MAJ)   **Aug 12 – Present**
Unit and Location

- Oversees the proper marking of over 500 classified documents to ensure compliance with exemption categories 1-9 of section 3.3, EO 13526.
- Identifies possible Nuclear Weapon delivery systems and other intelligence information, such as captured weapons, arms trafficking activities focused on the Middle East, Africa and the EUCOM AOR.
- Initiates hundreds of classified Source Directed Requirements and over 50 collection emphasis messages to ensure questions to collection assets are appropriately written to ensure Intelligence Gaps are answered.
- Warns Intelligence Community of destabilization activities.
- Final reviewer of analysis and synchronizes MS PowerPoint presentations, which includes eight Commands and up to 40 personnel.

EDUCATION

MA in Military History	School, Location (100 credit hours)(exp grad)	2016
BA in History	School, Location	1988
AA in Liberal Arts	School, Location	1985

TRAINING

MI Officer Basic Course	School, Location	2010
Intelligence in Combating Terrorism Course	School, Location	2010
Officer Candidate School	School, Location	2009
Small Group Instruction Course	School, Location	2009
Basic Instructor Training Course	School, Location	2008
Battle Staff Course	School, Location	2007
Safety Officer Course	School, Location	2006

OBJECTIVE FIRE

Target Your Résumé . When targeting your résumé to the vacancy announcement the most critical element to concentrate on is the top half of the first page. In this section, you must quickly identify to the hiring manager and recruiter that you are qualified for the job and meet all vacancy

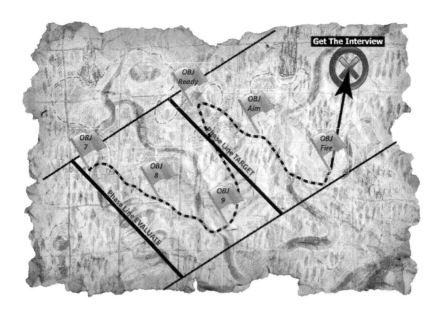

requirements, as well as years of experience in accordance with the vacancy announcement. Problems may arise because you tend to utilize the top half of your résumé to list all of your personal strengths. Although this is partially correct, it tends to overload the reader, because most of the information is not required within the vacancy announcement and, therefore, is not relevant to the announcement.

If you are one of many people who list all of your training, certifications, education, as well as an objective statement in the top half of the first page, then you have successfully started your autobiography and not a targeted résumé. In order to change this autobiography to a targeted résumé, you only should put those items that are REQUIRED by the vacancy announcement within the top first half of the first page of your résumé. These items normally consist of security clearance and the year adjudicated, the polygraph and the year taken, a Bachelor's and/or a Master's degree, and six to eight key words that are listed within the vacancy announcement.

In addition to this, somewhere in the top half of the first page, you should state the actual job title of the vacancy to which you are applying. This will ensure the hiring manager and recruiter understands immediately that your entire résumé is focused (Aimed) on this particular vacancy announcement; therefore, making this a targeted résumé.

Bruce Benedict, PMP
(MAJ/O4, US Army, Retired)

Address (XXX) 207-2716
Address Bruce@BattlefieldResumes.com

HIGHLIGHTS OF QUALIFICATIONS
TOP SECRET/SCI (2009), BA in HISTORY
Skilled **Declassification Analyst** *with experience and proficiency in the following:*

- Classification/Declassification Guides
- Exemption Cat. 1-9, Sec 3.3, EO13526
- Classified Document Marking Procedures
- Unclassified & Classified Document Analysis
- Nuclear Weapon Identification

PROFESSIONAL EXPERIENCE

Intelligence Analyst (MAJ) **Aug 12 – Present**
Unit and Location
- Oversees the proper marking of over 500 classified documents to ensure compliance with exemption categories 1-9 of section 3.3, EO 13526.
- Identifies possible Nuclear Weapon delivery systems and other intelligence information, such as captured weapons, arms trafficking activities focused on the Middle East, Africa and the EUCOM AOR.
- Initiates hundreds of classified Source Directed Requirements and over 50 collection emphasis messages to ensure questions to collection assets are appropriately written to ensure Intelligence Gaps are answered.
- Warns Intelligence Community of destabilization activities.
- Final reviewer of analysis and synchronizes MS PowerPoint presentations, which includes eight Commands and up to 40 personnel.

EDUCATION

MA in Military History	School, Location (100 credit hours)(exp grad)	2016
BA in History	School, Location	1988
AA in Liberal Arts	School, Location	1985

TRAINING

MI Officer Basic Course	School, Location	2010
Intelligence in Combating Terrorism Course	School, Location	2010
Officer Candidate School	School, Location	2009
Small Group Instruction Course	School, Location	2009
Basic Instructor Training Course	School, Location	2008
Battle Staff Course	School, Location	2007
Safety Officer Course	School, Location	2006

**OPERATIONS ORDER
MESSAGE**

Congratulations! You have successfully accomplished all 12 objectives within all four phases of the operation. You have successfully hit the target with your tailored and targeted résumé, anxiously awaiting a call from the hiring manager for an interview…

Good Luck,
BB

CHAPTER 8

THE ENEMY'S PERSPECTIVE OF YOU

Avenue of Approach

"IF YOU KNOW THE ENEMY AND KNOW YOURSELF, YOU NEED NOT FEAR THE RESULT OF A HUNDRED BATTLES. IF YOU KNOW YOURSELF BUT NOT THE ENEMY, FOR EVERY VICTORY GAINED YOU WILL ALSO SUFFER A DEFEAT. IF YOU KNOW NEITHER THE ENEMY NOR YOURSELF, YOU WILL SUCCUMB IN EVERY BATTLE."
(SUN TZU, THE ART OF WAR)

Résumé Strategy. Let's take a closer look at the résumé format and let's walk through the hiring manager's analysis and evaluation phases, since they are integral parts of your successful résumé strategy. In order to make sure you completely understand the methodology, can incorporate the methodology into your strategy and can apply the methodology to different types of battlefields/ vacancy announcements, you will need to break down the following résumé into the enemy's/hiring manager's Phase Lines. What does this mean? This will show you the method by which the hiring manager will read your résumé. It will establish the order in which Areas of Interests within your résumé are normally read; how your résumé can be modified to implement a strategy, and ensure the appropriate information is correctly conveyed. In doing this, you will validate your résumé calibration and that you actually hit the target.

The enemy/hiring manager spends approximately six seconds on each résumé to determine whether an individual is qualified in accordance with the vacancy announcement. Additionally, the enemy/hiring manager will also determine whether one applicant résumé is more qualified than other applicant résumés. If the applicant targeted his/her résumé directly to the vacancy announcement, the hiring manager will identify this immediately. Once identified, the hiring manager will accept the résumé as "qualified" and place the résumé into a "qualified" stack of résumés. On the other hand, if the applicant did not target their résumé to the vacancy announcement, the hiring manager will likely disqualify the résumé within their six-second review. The reason for this is that the résumé conveys to the hiring manager it does not meet the vacancy announcement requirements, or for other reasons such as not meeting the required years of experience, and will place the résumé in the "not qualified" stack.

Once the hiring manager screens all résumés, the hiring manager will return to the "qualified" stack of résumés and compare each résumé with the others to determine the top five to ten best qualified applicants. If the applicant tailored their résumé to the vacancy and quantified each bulleted statement with positive impacts/outcomes, as well as developed a proper résumé theme based on the vacancy announcement, that applicant will have the best chance of being contacted for an interview.

How can the Enemy determine if you are qualified if they only spend six seconds on your résumé? This is a great question and one that will be answered in this chapter. In order to develop a résumé that the hiring manager would like to see, you must first understand how most hiring managers read your résumé. For starters, put yourself in the hiring manager's position and look at the following résumé. The first thing the hiring manager does is review your résumé from the top down. This, you could say, is the enemy's Avenue of Approach.

Next, since you must assume that the hiring manager wrote the vacancy announcement and is intimately familiar with its requirements, they will always have those requirements on their mind while reading your résumé. Therefore, the direction of attack by the enemy/hiring manager immediately starts from the top of the résumé, working through the center of the top half of the first page of the résumé. You will title this area of your résumé by the name Highlighted Qualifications. These are highlighted qualifications based on the requirements within the vacancy announcement, not based on the applicant's strengths. The applicant's strengths are not always the same as the vacancy announcement requirements.

The hiring manager, as he/she reads your résumé, will immediately recognize whether or not you are qualified for the job. Therefore, you must place the top six to eight requirements and key words in this section to convey immediately to the hiring manager that you are qualified for the position and that he/she should read your résumé further.

Many applicants encounter problems based on their strategy within this area of interest. If an applicant's strategy is to extract all of their key strengths and place them inside this section, they will continue to be unsuccessful in getting an interview. Why is this, you may ask? Because they have not calibrated their weapon appropriately and have not tailored or targeted their résumé to the vacancy announcement, but only developed an autobiography of their skills. Therefore, not providing the hiring manager with the necessary information up front to make an immediate, six-second decision as to their qualifications will result in mission failure.

In the following résumé example, the hiring manager can quickly see that the applicant meets the key requirements of the vacancy announcement. The requirements are identified in the top half of the first page as follows: top secret clearance, a bachelor's degree, classification declassification guide, exemption categories, classified document marking procedures, unclassified and classified document analysis, records management, intelligence information, strong research and analytical skills and strong verbal and written communication.

Another key element within this section of the résumé is the title of the position for which the applicant is applying. This strategy is extremely important in order to convey immediately to the hiring manager for which job your résumé is targeting.

OPERATION: CIVILIAN RÉSUMÉ

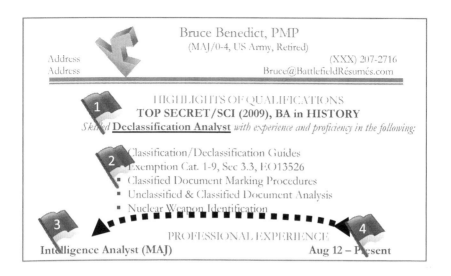

In a matter of one to two seconds, the hiring manager *analyzes* and interprets the top half of your résumé as qualified (or not qualified) for the position. At this point in the process the hiring manager places your résumé in the respective stack of résumés for later review and comparison. One further note, always place your military retired rank, or the last rank held while in the military, just below the applicant's name. The reason for this, unlike the private sector, is that in defense contracting, many employers are prior military and their announced positions are normally related to the Department of Defense. Therefore, listing your rank under your name will immediately convey many assumptions as to your experience, training and leadership.

Next, and almost instantaneously, the enemy/hiring manager will *analyze* the battlefield to look for patterns of activity throughout the areas of interest. Therefore, you must ensure your job titles are developed with a theme in mind that directly supports the Highlighted Qualifications within your résumé. As well, your job titles should immediately convey what your duties and responsibilities were for the targeted vacancy announcement. Many transitioning military members often have an ethical dilemma in modifying their job titles and appear to be personally attached to their job titles. This is an obstacle that you will have to maneuver around in order to achieve your objectives and a successful mission. However, keep in mind that the enemy does not translate military jargon and, therefore, may not understand what your actual title means. For example, if you were the S3 OIC, the enemy may not understand what this title means or what your actual duties were.

Therefore, you need to modify your job titles to something that better aligns to the vacancy announcement as well as your actual duties/responsibilities.

However, in using this same strategy…if you are applying to a vacancy announcement that actually states that they are looking for or have a requirement for someone who has worked as an "S3 OIC," then your job title should remain "S3 OIC," thereby directly aligning to the vacancy announcement requirement. Keeping a tailored/targeted job title theme throughout your résumé will convey to the hiring manager that you have more experience than other applicants, therefore putting you on the top of the qualified résumé stack.

As the hiring manager quickly scans your tailored/targeted job titles, he/she will ultimately look to the back page for additional education, training and/or certifications section of your résumé. If your education, training and certifications are formatted appropriately, the hiring manager will quickly scan them, and conclude whether or not your experience was based on the proper standardized education, training or certification. If so, you are more qualified than other applicants who do not have associated experience.

However, if you don't have associated education, training or certifications that support your experience, you run the risk of your résumé conveying that you may have developed bad habits throughout your continued experiences. Remember, if the vacancy announcement requires specific education, training or certifications, you must also add these required elements to the Highlighted Qualifications section on the first page. Additionally, if you have higher level certifications or education, such as a PhD, MBA, CISSP, CPA, etc. It is recommended that you place these titles behind your name to ensure they are recognized immediately.

OPERATION: CIVILIAN RÉSUMÉ

PROFESSIONAL EXPERIENCE

Intelligence Analyst (MAJ)　　　　　　　　　　　　　Aug - Present
Unit and Location
- Oversees the proper marking of over 500 classified documents to ensure compliance with exemption categories 1-9 of section 3.3, EO 13526.
- Identifies possible Nuclear Weapon delivery systems and other intelligence information, such as captured weapons, arms trafficking activities focused on the Middle East, Africa and the EUCOM AOR.
- Initiates hundreds of classified Source Directed Requirements and over 50 Warns Intelligence Community of destabilization activities.
- Final reviewer of analysis and synchronizes MS PowerPoint presentations, which includes eight Commands and up to 40 personnel.

EDUCATION

MA in Military History	School, Location (100 credit hours)(exp grad)	2016
BA in History	School, Location	1988
AA in Liberal Arts	School, Location	1985

TRAINING

MI Officer Basic Course	School, Location	2010
Intelligence in Combating Terrorism Course	School, Location	2010
Officer Candidate School	School, Location	2009
Small Group Instruction Course	School, Location	2009
Basic Instructor Training Course	School, Location	2008
Battle Staff Course	School, Location	2007
Safety Officer Course	School, Location	2006

At this point, the hiring manager has now scanned your résumé in six seconds and has determined that your résumé belongs in the "qualified" résumé stack. Now it's time for the hiring manager to *evaluate* your résumé against all other qualified applicants. The hiring manager will now evaluate each "area of interest" (job titles/dates, etc), calculating how many total years the applicant has worked in the required areas to ensure the applicant is qualified to work on the contract for which they are hiring. These qualifications are aligned to the requirements within the government contract for which the hiring manager is hiring and are normally aligned to salary levels. Therefore, it is extremely important for applicants to place their dates of experience as clearly and concisely as possible by using the month and year format.

At this time, the hiring manager will evaluate at least the first two or three bullets within each job assignment listed in your résumé. Therefore, to ensure your résumé conveys better experience to the vacancy announcement than other applicants, you must make sure that the first, second and, often times, third bullet within each work experience directly supports the job title and, more importantly, the Highlighted Qualifications" of your résumé.

PROFESSIONAL EXPERIENCE

Intelligence Analyst   **Aug 12 – Present**
Unit and Location
- Oversees the processing of over 500 classified documents to ensure compliance with exemption categories 1-9 of section 3.3, EO 13526.
- Identifies possible Nuclear Weapon delivery systems and other intelligence information, such as captured weapons, arms trafficking activities focused on the Middle East, Africa and the EUCOM AOR.
- Initiates hundreds of classified Source Directed Requirements and over 50 Warns Intelligence Community of destabilization activities.
- Final reviewer of analysis and synchronizes MS PowerPoint presentations, which includes eight Commands and up to 40 personnel.

EDUCATION

MA in Military History	School, Location (100 credit hours)(exp grad)	2016
BA in History	School, Location	1988
AA in Liberal Arts	School, Location	1985

TRAINING

To ensure the applicant is highly qualified and in need of an interview, the hiring manager will evaluate the first three bullets of each work experience for quantifiable details and positive accomplishments. The hiring manager will feel more confident that you have the required experience necessary for the position if these first two to three bullets intuitively support the respective job title and key words listed in the Highlighted Qualifications (as shown in the following example). The hiring manager will ultimately compare these quantifiable details and positive accomplishments with other applicants, identifying those five to ten individuals that have the potential to bring value to their company.

Remember, the hiring manager interprets your past performance and accomplishments, as listed within your résumé, as an indicator of potential. Similar to the military, your past successes are indicators of future performance and, therefore, will be expected from you in your future position.

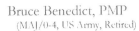

Bruce Benedict, PMP
(MAJ/O-4, US Army, Retired)

Address   (XXX) 207-2716
Address   Bruce@BattlefieldRésumés.com

HIGHLIGHTS OF QUALIFICATIONS
TOP SECRET/SCI (2009), BA in HISTORY
Skilled **Declassification Analyst** *with experience and proficiency in the following:*

- Classification/Declassification Guides
- Exemption Cat. 1-9, Sec 3.3, EO 13526
- Classified Document Marking Procedures
- Unclassified & Classified Document Analysis
- Nuclear Weapon Identification

PROFESSIONAL EXPERIENCE
Intelligence Analyst   **Aug 12 – Present**
Unit and Location

➢ Oversees the proper marking of over 500 classified documents to ensure compliance with exemption categories 1-9 of section 3.3, EO 13526.
➢ Identifies possible Nuclear Weapon delivery systems and other intelligence information, such as captured weapons, arms trafficking activities focused on the Middle East, Africa and the EUCOM AOR.

In summary, please look at the enemy's complete Avenue of Approach in the following résumé and observe how he/she will scan a résumé, maneuvering to each area of interest within the résumé. Additionally, look how the enemy starts from the top of your résumé, initially maneuvering through the Highlighted Qualifications to quickly determine if your résumé is worth perusing further, then coming back to the same area to confirm that your qualifications align to the vacancy announcement. Once you have completed these activities and developed your own tailored and targeted résumé based on your Intelligence Preparation of the battlefield and your predictive analysis of the enemy's avenue of approach to each area of interest, you can then exploit the enemy's predictable maneuvers. If done correctly, the hiring manager will have no other option than to categorize your résumé as one of the highly qualified applicants and invite you for an interview.

Please see the résumé on the following page that identifies the entire route of the enemy on the battlefield as well as your targets.

OPERATION: CIVILIAN RÉSUMÉ

MESSAGE

Congratulations! You have successfully accomplished all objectives and phases for a properly targeted résumé. You have calibrated your résumé based on the Intelligence Preparation of the Battlefield and predicted the enemy's intentions and methods when reviewing your résumé.

Good Luck,
BB

Bruce Benedict, PMP
(MAJ/O-4, US Army, Retired)

Address (XXX) 207-2716
Address Bruce@BattlefieldResumés.com

HIGHLIGHTS OF QUALIFICATIONS
TOP SECRET/SCI (2009), BA in HISTORY
Skilled Declassification Analyst with experience and proficiency in the following:

- Classification/Declassification Guides
- Exemption Cat. 1-9 Sec 3.3, EO13526
- Classified Document Marking Procedures
- Unclassified & Classified Document Analysis
- Nuclear Weapon Identification

PROFESSIONAL EXPERIENCE
Intelligence Analyst (MAJ) Aug 12 – Present
Unit, Location
- Oversees the proper marking of over 500 classified documents to ensure compliance with exemption categories 1-9 of section 3.3, EO 13526.
- Identifies possible Nuclear Weapon delivery systems and other intelligence information, such as captured weapons, arms trafficking activities focused on the Middle East, Africa and the EUCOM AOR.
- Initiates hundreds of classified Source Directed Requirements and over 50 collection emphasis messages to ensure questions to collection assets are appropriately written to ensure Intelligence Gaps are answered.
- Warns Intelligence Community of destabilization activities.
- Final reviewer of analysis and synchronizes MS PowerPoint presentations, which include eight Commands and up to 40 personnel.

EDUCATION
MA in Military History	School, Location (100 credit hours)(exp grad)	2016
BA in History	School, Location	1988
AA in Liberal Arts	School, Location	1985

TRAINING
MI Officer Basic Course	School, Location	2010
Individual in Combating Terrorism Course	School, Location	2010
Officer Candidate School	School, Location	2009
Small Group Instruction Course	School, Location	2009
Basic Instructor Training Course	School, Location	2008
Battle Staff Course	School, Location	2007
Safety Officer Course	School, Location	2006

CHAPTER 9

REHEARSAL

Wargame Practice

"TO KNOW YOUR ENEMY, YOU MUST BECOME YOUR ENEMY."
(SUN TZU, THE ART OF WAR)

Now, like in all missions, you must rehearse what you have learned. A rehearsal is one of the most important elements to proper preparation. In order to prepare for your mission, you must practice analyzing vacancy announcements and résumés. In this chapter, you will analyze four vacancy announcements and four résumés to ensure you are ready for combat (answers are listed in appendix A).

It's time to put what you learned into practice. In the following four vacancy announcements, you must identify the mandatory requirements, analyze job descriptions and analyze the key words and patterns that the hiring manager may have developed. Highlight each area as you have been trained and review each respective résumé.

After analyzing each vacancy announcement, you must then analyze the associated résumé. Think of yourself as the hiring manager who must review each résumé and determine if the applicant meets the vacancy requirements and, therefore, deserves an interview. Use what you have just learned and maneuver through each résumé using enemy tactics. Refer back to your notes to ensure you can identify the requirements, key words and theme within each résumé.

PRACTICE 1

1. Analyze the vacancy announcement. (Draw your avenue of approach and objectives directly on the vacancy announcement if needed.)
2. List the vacancy requirements and the key words.
3. Review the résumé as if you are the Hiring Manager.
4. Identify the Hiring Manager Avenue of Approach, then highlight where the vacancy requirements and key words are located. (Draw the enemy's avenue of approach and objectives directly on the résumé if needed.)

Practice Vacancy 1

X Company is seeking a seasoned Project Manager for a project at a client site in City, State, US operating in a fast-paced, high-energy, stimulating, challenging, and rewarding environment. The successful candidate will:

- Lead a software development team comprised of X Company Software employees
- Manage integrated project teams and initiatives comprised of resources from multiple companies
- Manage multiple project initiatives at once, and maintain flexibility to adjust priorities according to client needs
- Demonstrate understanding of full SDLC
- Have working knowledge of various project management methodologies
- Have working knowledge of project management tools (Microsoft Project, SharePoint, Project Server, HP Quality Center, etc.)
- Interface with client on a daily and continuous basis
- Exercise judgment and diplomacy working with the client, customer, team personnel, and personnel from other entities
- Maintain a polished, professional deportment while representing the company to the client, and while representing the client to other project stakeholders
- Function as a genuine leader for company personnel, providing solid direction, encouragement, coaching, discipline, and at times a lifeline
- Function as a tether between project team and corporate headquarters, maintaining a candid, open, ongoing discussion of project disposition with executive management
- Provide daily project updates as well as weekly status reports
- Conduct team personnel performance reviews and manage a salary budget pool

Position requirements:

Minimum 5 years of experience performing full-time project management and project team leadership; Minimum 10 years overall professional experience; Project management of software development teams highly preferred, but not required; Current PMP credential (or able to obtain it within 6 months) Agile and/or ITIL certifications helpful, but not required.

NOTES:

Identify the Mandatory Requirements:

_____
_____
_____
_____
_____

Analyze the Job Description:

_____
_____
_____
_____
_____

Identify the Key Words:

_____
_____
_____
_____
_____

OPERATION: CIVILIAN RÉSUMÉ

Practice Résumé 1

Bruce Benedict, MBA, PMP
(Major/O-4, US Army, Retired)

Address (XXX) 207-2716
Address Bruce@BattlefieldRésumés.com

HIGHLIGHTS OF QUALIFICATIONS

TS/SCI (Feb 2013), CI SCOPE POLYGRAPH (2008), MBA, PMP (2009)
Skilled Senior Project Manager *with strong proficiency and experience in the following:*

- ITIL v3 Expert
- Integrated Project Teams
- 29 yrs Project Management
- 29 yrs Project Team Leadership
- Budget Management
- Software Life Cycle Development
- Project Management Methodologies
- MS Project, Project, Server and Excel

PROFESSIONAL EXPERIENCE

Project Manager, Integrated Schedule Manager Mar 11 - May 13
Organization, City, State
- Used Microsoft (MS) Project to track 6 concurrent, major system development programs, containing 1000 – 2500 tasks. Data from these programs were placed into an overall Integrated Master Schedule (IMS).
- Prepared detailed change reports for each integrated schedule, validating predicted milestone dates through critical path analysis of development through installation.
- Briefed customer on potential resource and personnel schedule conflicts among several concurrent system development and installation efforts, including ad hoc analyses and reports to include forecasts.
- Identifying a previously unknown development problem with a circuit card in the integrated master schedule data, revealing a retest not identified by the developer.

Project Manager, Budget / Financial Management Nov 08 - Mar 11
Organization, City, State
- Researched and drafted the response to a Congressional inquiry about the agency's IT budget, draft comments had minimal changes prior to release to Congress.
- Facilitated the Office of Management and Budget's (OMB) requirement to review and evaluate IT spending across the Federal Government, ensured information for several agencies was correct in the Federal IT Investment Portfolio, which is part of the President's Budget.
- Identified discrepancies and drafted critical corrections for the annual Enterprise Roadmap submission to OMB, information technology summary data within the Agency IT Investment Portfolio (Exhibit 53) and the IT Capital Asset Summary (Exhibit 300). Multiple high-level reports were reconciled.
- Conducted Alternative Analysis, Benefit-Cost Analysis, the Business Reference Model (BRM) and Service Reference Model (SRM) of the Federal Enterprise Architecture (FEA) for agency-level reviews of planned initiatives that were part of a Budget Estimate Submission (BES).

Project Manager   May 04 - Nov 08
Organization, City, State
- Customer witness for hardware and software integration testing at the factory and at operational locations, addressing specific areas of concern to program COTR.
- Site manager recognized the verification method used as innovative and for helping to keep a six-month network installation on schedule
- Coordinated the review of test plans, test procedures and reports that facilitated timely Government responses with little exception.
- Test witness also for a major post-installation, multi-system test and tracked requirement verification for customer test lead. Work received recognition by senior managers.
- Reduced program risk by developing a Microsoft Access database and procedures to use with the Requirements Traceability Management (RTM) tool, auditing approx. 3300 system requirements

Project Manager, Contract / CDRL Management   May 03 – May 04
Organization, City, State
- Prepared Basis of Estimates (BOE) that provided several thousand labor hours and other direct costs for a successful classified program proposal, receiving a performance award for this successful effort.
- Coordinated the review, provided feedback to the customer to the Government and kept the status of several hundred Contract Data Requirements List (CDRL) submittals
- Analyzed and identified CDRLs that had outdated information or CDRLs that provided redundant information. These CDRLs were removed from the follow-on contract saving about $50,000 each.
- Assisted contracting officer in executing the withdrawal of out-dated CDRL submittals.

Project Manager, Portfolio Management   Aug 98 – Mar 03
Organization, City, State
- Briefed Assistant Director to the CIO on the results of an IT portfolio benchmark analysis and the results of a market surveys for commercially available portfolio management tools - all recommendations accepted
- Defined semi-annual portfolio management process to manage the portfolio of several business IT systems, synchronizing the process to the annual Planning, Programming and Budget System (PPBS) cycle.
- Researched technical merits and cost of individual projects using business cases that were based on the Exhibit 300. Provided recommendations to the senior managers of the Investment Review Board for IT.
- Prepared 3 Congressionally-mandated semi-annual reports that provided the status of a business transformation program of record to four standing Congressional committees.

EDUCATION

MBA – (school, location)	1992
BS in Organizational Behavior – (school, location)	1986

TRAINING

Program Management Office Course	2004
DoD Acquisition Course	1989

CERTIFICATIONS

Information Technology Infrastructure Library (ITIL) v3 Expert	2013
Project Management Professional (PMP), Program Management Institute	2003

PRACTICE 2

1. Analyze the vacancy announcement. (Draw your avenue of approach and objectives directly on the vacancy announcement if needed.)
2. List the vacancy requirements and the key words.
3. Review the résumé as if you are the Hiring Manager.
4. Identify the Hiring Manager Avenue of Approach, then highlight where the vacancy requirements and key words are located. (Draw the enemy's avenue of approach and objectives directly on the résumé if needed.)

Practice Vacancy 2

Counter Terrorism Analyst
Description:
The Mission Support Business Unit has a career opportunity for a CT/AT/FP Analyst at City, State, US. This position will provide focus for analytical efforts for regional and transnational terrorist and insurgent organizations; conduct threat assessments and vulnerability assessments of critical infrastructure pertaining to specific, potential threats in the Pacific Command (PACOM) Area of Responsibility (AOR); construct and deliver daily and weekly briefings, provide all-source analysis, conduct research, and author papers as requested to support the Command regarding issues relevant to the security of the United States and forces within the PACOM AOR as requested by the Government staff or contractor site lead; provide Counter-Terrorism (CT) threat assessments, travel briefings, and force protection support to deploying units, groups, and individuals who are traveling to various countries on leave, exercise-support, or real-world missions and provide the Command with a daily update of deployed personnel and projected deployment dates of all personnel; maintain and update the CT assessments and briefs on the G2 Operations travel briefs website/portal which will include the country threat, cultural awareness issues, and travel precautions and best practices; provide input to the Commanding General's daily read book and associated briefings; assist the G2 with organizing and providing subject matter expertise to the Threat Working Group and the Anti-Terrorism Working Group meetings and maintain situational awareness of political, economic, diplomatic, criminal, military, and terrorism-related developments; and provide exercise support, perform periodic shift work and to travel within the PACOM AOR and other CONUS locations.

Qualifications:
A Bachelor's degree in Liberal Arts/Sciences (or related field) and/or equivalent formal military training and 6 years related experience including work in all-source analysis environments with emphasis on CT, CI, AT and FP. An additional 4 years of related work experience may be considered in lieu of the Bachelor's degree. Must have a thorough understanding of the U.S. Intelligence Community, the intelligence cycle, processes and organizations as they relate to counter terrorism analysis.

Desired Qualifications
Prior experience in CT/CI/FP/AT analysis of terrorist and insurgent organizations in the PACOM area of responsibility.

Job Posting: Feb 15, 2013, 8:28:22 AM

NOTES:

Identify the Mandatory Requirements:

_____

_____

_____

_____

_____

Analyze the Job Description:

_____

_____

_____

_____

_____

Identify the Key Words:

_____

_____

_____

_____

_____

Practice Résumé 2

Bruce Benedict
(SFC/E7, US Army, Retired)

Address (XXX) 207-2716
Address Bruce@BattlefieldRésumés.com

HIGHLIGHTS OF QUALIFICATIONS

TOP SECRET/SCI (2011), MASTER'S DEGREE in Intelligence Studies
Skilled Counterterrorism (CT) Analyst with strong experience and proficiency in the following:

- CT/AT/FP Analysis
- Threat Assessments
- Vulnerability Assessments
- Critical Infrastructure
- All-Source Analyst
- Travel Briefings
- PACOM AOR
- Exercise Support

PROFESSIONAL EXPERIENCE

CT/AT/FP Senior Intelligence Analyst Nov 10 - Jan 13
Organization, City, State
- Reviewed and produced all-source Counterterrorism, Anti-terrorism, Force Protection (CT/AT/FP) intelligence products within the division of six personnel; provided critical intelligence assessments of developing threats to the base to ensure U.S. and local security units were able to accurately determine appropriate force protection postures during real-world and exercise scenarios.
- Formulated 3 base vulnerability assessments utilizing geospatial intelligence systems, human intelligence and counterintelligence (CI) reporting; provided approximately 15 page operational base assessments identifying physical structure, criminal, and terrorist vulnerabilities for base commanders and force protection forces to address strategies for mitigating base threats.
- Conducted threat and vulnerability assessments on regional and transnational terrorist organizations supporting Air Force in providing CT threat assessments of possible extremist groups residing in the PACOM AOR and review of intelligence information reports (IIRs); ensured case officers had the tailored intelligence to support counterintelligence operations.

CT/AT/FP Intelligence Superintendent Sep 07 - Nov 10
Organization, City, State
- Conducted pre-travel briefings for personnel traveling throughout the PACOM AOR; identified political, economic, diplomatic, criminal, military and terrorism-related developments to travelers and deployers; ensured FP package time line and security requirements for compliance with PACOM AT/FP travel program were met--no personnel loss or incidents.
- Integrated intelligence operations to produce 80 CT/AT/FP threat assessments and intelligence participation in special Threat Working Groups.

- Received "Excellent" ratings for Inspector General compliance and operational readiness inspections for its operations in research, coordination with local and federal security teams, medical units, and foreign security teams.
- Provided force protection recommendations to unit commanders and deployed teams within the PACOM AOR.
- Oversaw the development of intelligence support to force protection operations IAW policies and regulations to support the group's real-world deployments and exercise scenarios.
- Ensure timely CT/AT/FP strategy and response planning for 758-manned unit by monitoring and reporting threat situations to the commander, staff, and deployed personnel regarding critical political, military, and terrorism related issues and capabilities to; provided daily situational updates on PACOM AOR and its operational impacts on deployed assets.

Sr. All-Source Analyst   Jul 04 - Sep 07
Organization, City, State
- Oversaw the production of intelligence to identify illicit trafficking, internal security measures, threat networks and key personalities involved in narcotics production, trafficking, and related criminal and terrorism financing or operations to support theater- and national-level counternarcotics and CT missions.
- Applied advanced intelligence collection and production concepts, principles, practices, laws, regulations, methods, and techniques to provide counter narco-terrorism intelligence products for U.S. and host-nation counternarcotics and CT forces.
- Supervised and managed the division of 6 personnel leading all-source collection management and intelligence operations team providing collection requirements management and HUMINT and IMINT production, interpretation, analysis, and dissemination of national intelligence products in support of counterdrug assessments and operations.

Collection Manager, HUMINT   Dec 02 - Jul 04
Organization, City, State
- Authored, prioritized and validated standing (long-term) and ad hoc (short-term) HUMINT collection requirements to joint, national, theater and organic collections assets in support of COCOM Priority Intelligence Requirements and AT/FP requirements.

Indications & Warning (I&W) Analyst   Apr 01 - Dec 02
Organization, City, State
- Conducted CT and AT/FP intelligence warning and assessments to commanders and deployed personnel to ensure commanders were able to execute appropriate FP postures to protect personnel and assets.

- Ensured the timely I&W support of over 9000 airlift and sealift missions in support of Operations Enduring Freedom by reviewing and managing the screening of over 2000 messages per day and providing relevant AT/FP intelligence to command planners and operators.
- I&W Watch Shift NCOIC; led fused multi-source reporting on existing or pending military and terrorism threats to the COCOM and component personnel and assets operating worldwide.

EDUCATION

MA, Intelligence Studies (school, location)	2013
BS, Management/Human Resources, (school, location)	2003
AA, General Studies, (school, location)	2001
AAS, Communications Applications Technology, (school, location)	2000
AAS, Logistics, (school, location)	1998

TRAINING

CI Missions and Functions	2011
Enlisted Intelligence Master Skills	2010
Strategic Debriefing of Law Enforcement Sources	2007
J2X (CI/HUMINT) Operations Course	2007
Joint Collection Management	2006
Intelligence, Surveillance, & Reconnaissance Fundamentals	2005
Intelligence Collection Course	2005
Intelligence Support to Force Protection	2005
Joint Combined Interagency Intelligence	2004
Warning Analysis	2002
Joint Intelligence Analyst Course	2001
All-Source Analyst Course	1996

PRACTICE 3

1. Analyze the vacancy announcement. (Draw your avenue of approach and objectives directly on the vacancy announcement if needed.)
2. List the vacancy requirements and the key words.
3. Review the résumé as if you are the Hiring Manager.
4. Identify the Hiring Manager Avenue of Approach, then highlight where the vacancy requirements and key words are located. (Draw the enemy's avenue of approach and objectives directly on the résumé if needed.)

Practice Vacancy 3

Our computer forensics professionals analyze digital media and evidence providing detailed analysis to help uncover essential facts and insights. We can bring to bear the range of our forensic investigation skill set to help our clients with their investigations. We have developed methodologies and strategies that help clients handle difficult circumstances.

Description:

· Function as investigative resource; provide technical expertise while also learning the use of utilizing cutting edge tools and techniques to extract, analyze and report on captured data

· Perform accurate analysis and effective diagnosis of client issues and manage day-to-day client relationships at peer client levels.

· Assist in proposal development, as requested.

Required Skills:

- Minimum of 5 years of experience industry experience
- Ability to work independently and manage multiple task assignments
- Demonstrated expertise in computer forensics
- Willingness to travel both within the U.S. and internationally per client needs
- Bachelor's degree from an accredited four-year institution
- Expertise with the Microsoft operating system internals (e.g., registry, file formats, common artifact locations)
- Demonstrated knowledge of industry-standard computer forensics software and hardware
- Willingness to work in criminal investigations and provide expert testimony

· Secret security clearance

Preferred Skills:

· Moderate oral and written communication skills, including presentation skills (MS Visio, MS PowerPoint)

· Proficiency with Microsoft Excel and Word

· Problem solving and troubleshooting skills with the ability to exercise mature judgment

· Experience in criminal investigations

· Industry certifications, including CFCE, CCE, EnCE, ACE, GCFA, GCFE.

· Expertise with non-Microsoft operating systems (e.g., OS X, Linux, iOS, Android)

NOTES:

Identify the Mandatory Requirements:

_____

_____

_____

_____

Analyze the Job Description:

_____

_____

_____

_____

Identify the Key Words:

_____

_____

_____

_____

Practice Résumé 3

Bruce Benedict
MBA, PMP, CISSP

(XXX) 207-2716   Bruce@BattlefieldRésumé.com

HIGHLIGHTS OF QUALIFICATIONS

TOP SECRET (2009), MBA & MASTERS Degree in Information Systems
Skilled <u>Computer Forensics Professional</u> with strong experience and proficiency in the following:

- Encase, FTK, Paraben
- CHFI, EC_ECSA (Projected 2013)
- CISSP, CEH, MCSE, Net+, CCNA
- Nessus, eRetina, AppDetective, PGP, SRR

- Investigations
- NIST SP 800 series
- SAP, Oracle
- MCT, CTT

PROFESSIONAL EXPERIENCE

Sr. Cyber Information Systems Auditor   Dec 12 - Apr 13
Organization, City, State
- Scrutinizes digital evidence within Symantec Endpoint. Created a logical image with FTK to gain an understanding of the evidence.
- Discovered normal files, returned deleted files to their original state.
- Crafted five NIST 800 53 Series policies including Incident Response Policies and Procedures, Responds to and investigates potential incidents to rule out false positives, validate and search for forensic evidence. Created logical images with FTK and determined false positive.
- Performs gap analysis for the Department's GSS and NIST 800-53A Rev 3 series of 17 families of controls. Recommended a patch policy.

Sr. Cyber Security Consultant   Dec 11 - Dec 12
Organization, City, State
- Consulted on forensic reports and all security issues with CIO's and CEOs of other Cyber Security SBA organizations.
- Evaluated and analyzed the security profile of the CMS network infrastructure in relationship to the NIST 800-53A Rev 3 control family, including the output of the vulnerability scans. The results provided a recommendation for the Authority to Operate for the system.
- Served as a Cyber-Security and technical Subject Matter Expert for all related security investigations.
- Managed relationships with federal partners. Briefed trends to DoD and federal government officials and corporate executives.

Sr. Cyber Security and Privacy Consultation   Nov 09 - Dec 11
Organization, City, State
- Extracted, analyzed and presented complex web application vulnerabilities, including Cross Site Scripting and SQL injections for applications in the development for the Department.

- Detected potential attack vectors, by identifying persistent cookies with user names embedded in them.
- Developed process of implementing non-forensically acceptable tools to expedite an Encase investigation.
- Analyzed the Medicare Network through interviewing four different groups of key stakeholders and evaluating technical, operational and management controls.
- Led the team with approximately 14 people in the resolution of Project Objectives and Milestones for GSS.
- Analyzed client's security issues on the Medicare contract.

Sr. Cyber Information System Security Engineer, Manager   Jan 08 - Nov 09
Organization, City, State
- Analyzed detailed results of an audit, and led a team of 10 people in the resolution of over 650 findings for the eVerify Information System leading to an ATO and 13 Project Objectives and Milestones.
- Created and implemented a plan for network security architecture for delivery of a private cloud infrastructure to federal clients.
- Created Statement of Work for multiple contracts.

Sr Cyber Security Engineer   Jul 07 - Jan 08
Organization, City, State
- Conducted vulnerability assessment testing and implemented tools for the Certification and Accreditation (C & A) package on assigned Military Health System sites utilizing DITSCAP & DIACAP guidelines. These included networks which required a CAC card.
- Conducted automated vulnerability scans using Retina Network Scanner, App Detective, and Production Gold Disks, security checklists and scripts for UNIX and Oracle 10g. The tests and interviews verified or identified deviations from the DoD requirements for the applicable Military Health System.
- Created and presented Reports and POA&Ms to the DAA

Cyber Quality Control Consultant   Dec 06 – Jul 07
Organization, City, State
- Conducted access control testing to insure appropriate permissions were in place as it related to financial applications supporting Federal Student Aid Loan processing; these included applications utilizing Java, C and C++.
- Monitored initiation, development, tests and implementation of software development lifecycle to identify and track risks qualitatively, and provided recommendations on corrective and preventative actions.
- Analyzed and reviewed requirements and security plans for Federal Student Aid GSS.
- Conducted Security Tests and Evaluation testing for major applications released into production.

OPERATION: CIVILIAN RÉSUMÉ

CISCO Project Lead   **Sep 01 - Dec 06**
Organization, City, State
- Established a successful CISCO curriculum.
- Instructed the MCSE courses leading students to an MCSE certification.

Microsoft Sr. Systems Engineer   **Feb 01 – Jun 01**
Organization, City, State
- Operated and managed the MS Exchange and MS Windows servers for DoD.
- Analyzed and recommended updates for UPS system, Evaluated and crafted Disaster Recovery plan and procedures. Participated in the creation of the SSAA and the System Security Plan.
- Managed day-to-day client activities.

EDUCATION

MBA, Finance	(school, location)	2005
MS, Information Systems	(school, location)	2000
BS, Biology	(school, location)	1998

TRAINING / CERTIFICATIONS

- CISSP
- CISM
- CEH
- MCSE
- Net+
- CCNA
- Encase
- FTK
- Paraben
- Nessus
- NMAP
- eRetina
- Production Gold Disk
- SRR
- Symantec Endpoint
- Websense

PRACTICE 4

1. Analyze the vacancy announcement. (Draw your avenue of approach and objectives directly on the vacancy announcement if needed.)
2. List the vacancy requirements and the key words.
3. Review the résumé as if you are the Hiring Manager.
4. Identify the Hiring Manager Avenue of Approach, then highlight where the vacancy requirements and key words are located. (Draw the enemy's avenue of approach and objectives directly on the résumé if needed.)

Practice Vacancy 4

Cyber Counterintelligence Analyst Job, Date: Apr 17, 2013
Location: City, State, US
Description: Serve as a counterintelligence (CI) specialist and provide subject matter expertise to IC members fulfilling their CI responsibilities. Respond to cyber-related CI, Information Assurance (IA), and security incidents and conduct computer forensic analysis of hardware, firmware, and software. Run forensic examinations and analysis on systems, networks, and digital multimedia as directed by the client and draft written reports. Apply knowledge and mastery of CI concepts, principles, and practices to plan and conduct a full range of CI support to operations, investigations, analysis, and CI services. Employ knowledge of CI functional areas and state-of-the-art technologies, analytical tools, and communications processes to act independently to support CI activities. Develop analytical processes and methods to support cyber CI investigations and CI analysis and production. Exercise knowledge of the appropriate directives, regulations, policies, and procedures necessary to independently perform and supervise technical and administrative CI functions. Liaise with senior members and staff of the supported agency and leadership and staff throughout the CI and law enforcement communities.

Basic Qualifications: 5+ years of experience as a credentialed special agent-5+ years of experience with intelligence analysis, including counterintelligence, counterterrorism, cyber, cyber security, computer forensics, and law enforcement missions-5+ years of experience with offensive CI operations or CI investigations-5+ years of experience with CI, LE, Cyber Security, computer forensics-5+ years of experience with intelligence community roles, responsibilities, organizations, and capabilities-TS/SCI clearance required-BA or BS degree required

Additional Qualifications: Experience with Palantir, Analyst Notebook, HOTR, M3, or similar network analysis and message dissemination systems-Knowledge of the organizations and functions of the DoD CI and HUMINT community-Knowledge of the Missile Defense Agency (MDA) and the Ballistic Missile Defense System (BMDS)-Knowledge of DoD 5240.21, DoD Instruction 5240.26, DoD Instruction 5240.23, US Public Law, and DoD intelligence oversight policy issuances-Knowledge of the structure, policies, and directives of national intelligence agencies and organizations-Ability to interact with military and civilian senior representatives of national intelligence agencies-Possession of excellent oral and written communication skills-Computer Forensics Certifications, including EnCase or Access Data FTK (Forensic Tool Kit)

Clearance: Applicants selected will be subject to a security investigation and may need to meet eligibility requirements for access to classified information; TS/SCI clearance is required.

NOTES:

Identify the Mandatory Requirements:

_____

_____

_____

_____

_____

Analyze the Job Description:

_____

_____

_____

_____

_____

Identify the Key Words:

_____

_____

_____

_____

_____

Practice Résumé 4 (Answer)

Bruce Benedict

(XXX) 207-2716   Bruce@BattlefieldRésumés.com

HIGHLIGHTS OF QUALIFICATIONS

TOP SECRET/SCI (2012), CI SCOPE POLYGRAPH (2009), MS Degree
Skilled **Cyber CI Special Agent** *with strong experience in the following:*

- Cyber Forensics SME
- CI/CT/LE Cyber Analysis
- Network incident response
- ASOC, MCC Collection
- CI Investigations

- Certified Ethical Hacker
- Certified Forensic Examiner
- Operating System/Network Analysis
- Wireshark, Snort, Encase, and FTK
- Forensics/Intrusion Analysis

PROFESSIONAL EXPERIENCE

Cyber Counterintelligence (CI) Special Agent   **Jul 09 - Present**
Organization, City, State
- Operates as a Subject Matter Expert (SME) in multiple capacities performing Enterprise-level cyber security operations, insider threat detection and investigation, cyber forensics, cyber threat analysis and cyber intelligence IAW DoDI S-5240.23.
- Conducts forensic analysis of classified and unclassified network computer systems pertaining to policy violations and network intrusions.
- Conducts and manages full scope Cyber CI investigations in addition to incident response, digital collections and examinations (dead box, live, mobile and network).
- Responds to Cyber incidents, including insider threat and network intrusions that involve Army computers in area of responsibility.

Cyber Intelligence Specialist-Operations   **Jun 02 - Jul 09**
Organization, City, State
- Cyber Subject Matter Expert (SME) in multiple capacities managing a BMDS Cyber security project covering security events, tools and techniques.
- Represented the organization at national-level US Government Joint Task Force cyber threat working groups as the resident subject matter expert.
- Planned, coordinated, and executed cyber collection operations utilizing best methodology while adhering to local and national-level operational and oversight guidelines.
- Liaised with cyber security personnel from public, private, and government sectors at cyber security conferences in North America, Europe, and Asia.
- Conducted targeted analysis on hacking, hacking tools, and hacking TTPs, which resulted in numerous information reports for network security community.

Technology Coordinator   Jun 02 - Jun 06
Organization, City, State
- Supervised division-level technology help desk personnel, network engineer/technology administrator.
- Managed user network shares and user accounts in active directory for a division of 1000 plus users.
- Collaborated with twelve regional technology directors from Hewlett Packard, Microsoft, and Sun Software to create Instructional Technology (IT) curriculum that was accepted and implemented for 4 divisions consisting of 3,800 students and 384 staff.
- Led complex change, approving technology budgets, managing and updating technology equipment, and training end users on numerous hardware and software.
- Taught graduate-level technology coursework on technology integration to on-site Masters cohort consisting of over 36 adult learners through the State's University system.

Technology Coordinator/Educator   Jun 99 - Jun 02
Organization, City, State
- Led technology integration into a school system such as managing technology budget, purchasing technology hardware and software, and teaching technology courses
- Managed network shares and user accounts on Windows 2000 network
- Served as school webmaster responsible for creating and maintaining website as well as providing website development courses to teaching and administrative staff
- Presented Technology Integration at an international Conference on Technology
- Trained over 40 staff members on hardware and software including: Microsoft products, Blackboard, Adobe, and Video Editing Software

OPERATION: CIVILIAN RÉSUMÉ

EDUCATION

MS in Digital Forensic Science, (school, location)	2014
MA in Leadership Studies & Educational Technology, (school, location)	2001
MS in Teaching Credential, (school, location)	1997
BA in International Relations, (school, location)	1993

TRAINING

Technical Training

Certified Ethical Hacker Training (CEH) V8, EC-Council	2013
Access Data Mobile Phone Examiner (MPE+)	2012
Encase 7 Basic Course	2012
Encase 7 Intermediate Course	2012
SANS 408 – Computer Forensic Investigations, Windows In-Depth	2012
FIWE-Forensics & Intrusions in Windows Environment	2011
WFE-Windows Forensics – Encase	2011
OUT-Online Undercover Techniques	2011
MCCU-Managing Computer Crime Units	2010
CAC-Cyber Analyst Course	2010
Introduction to Cyber Investigations	2010
CIRC-Computer Incident Response Course	2009
INCH-Introduction to Networks and Computers	2009
WetStone - Hacking Boot camp for Investigators	2008
Network Security + Course	2008
Certified Ethical Hacker Training (CEH) V5, EC-Council	2008
International Penetration Tester Training (IPT)	2008
Cyber Investigations Training, Computer Search and Seizure	2007
Managing and Maintaining a Microsoft Windows 2003 Server	2005
Creating websites with ASP.Net 2.0 with Visual Studio	2005

Military Intelligence Training

Military Counterintelligence Collection (MCC)	2010
Advanced Source Operations Course (ASOC)	2010
Strategic Debriefing Course (DSDC)	2007
Chinese Mandarin Course, Defense Language Institute (DLI)	1990
Counterintelligence Special Agent Course (CISAC)	1990

CERTIFICATIONS

Certified Ethical Hacker (CEH)	2013
GIAC/SANS Certified Forensic Examiner (GCFE)	2012
DOD Cyber Crime Investigator	2011
DOD Forensic Examiner	2011
DOD Digital Media Collector	2010

CHAPTER 10
MISSION ACCOMPLISHED
Interview Notification

"HE WHO KNOWS THESE THINGS, AND IN FIGHTING PUTS HIS KNOWLEDGE INTO PRACTICE, WILL WIN HIS BATTLES."
(SUN TZU, THE ART OF WAR)

Watch out for Battlefield Traps. To assess whether you have fallen into a battlefield trap, ask yourself the following question: Are you qualified for the job to which you are applying, yet never receive an interview notification or feedback from the recruiter/hiring manager? If the answer is yes, then you have fallen into a trap on the battlefield and need to re-group and re-focus on your battlefield objectives.

What are battlefield traps? Battlefield traps are described as follows:

1. Failure to focus the résumé on relevant requirements.
2. Failure to tailor and target the résumé appropriately.
3. Failure to concentrate on the interview instead of the job.
4. "Showing-off" experience by writing an autobiography.

Failure to focus on relevant requirements will lead to wasted time and effort by you and the hiring manager. Failure to tailor and target your résumé appropriately will convey to the hiring manager that you quickly put together a résumé with little thought or preparation. This lack of effort will only influence the hiring manager's decision not to interview you.

Developing a powerful résumé is up to you, and only you. You are the only one who can put forth the required effort needed to produce a "qualified" résumé for the job you want. However, the trap of an inaccurately zero'd and inaccurately aimed résumé rests solely on your shoulders.

Focus your Intelligence Preparation of the Battlefield effort on the vacancy announcement requirements, job description key words and patterns in order to influence your résumé. Analyze and evaluate as many vacancy announcements as you can to interpret positions that the contracting company and US Government need to fill. Once you have identified the key words and phrases, methods and patterns, you will definitely hit the target

The Job Interview. When developing your résumé, your mission must always be to get the job interview. If you are focused on obtaining a job via a résumé submission, you need to re-focus and re-zero your weapon/résumé and aim for the interview, not the job. Remember, you cannot win a war without winning its battles. If you focus all of your efforts on getting the interview, your résumé will convey your desires. Therefore, since most applicants concentrate too heavily on the job itself and not the interview, they fall into another trap on the battlefield and write their résumé in a manner that is meant to "show-off" their experiences. Instead of trying to prove to the hiring manager how good you were in past, try to show how qualified you are for future employment. If you focus your efforts on the objectives and phases identified in this workbook, focus on your immediate mission, tailor your résumé for each specific vacancy and ensure each résumé is targeted to each vacancy announcement, you will be successful in more battles than you can ever imagine.

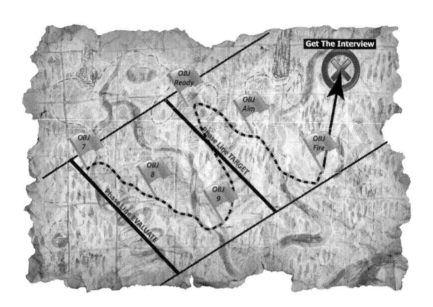

OPERATION: CIVILIAN RÉSUMÉ

MESSAGE

Congratulations! You have successfully calibrated your résumé, aimed your résumé upon the High Value Target and fired your weapon accurately. You have predicted enemy intent, recognized and used the enemy's methodology against them and studied the battlefield extensively. Based on your perseverance within each objective, you are now better prepared for each battle you encounter and now have the best chance at winning the war.

Good luck in your future battles and I wish you success in your future career,

BB

APPENDIX A
(PRACTICE ANSWERS)

PRACTICE 1 (ANSWER SHEET)

Practice Vacancy 1 (Answers)

X Company is seeking a seasoned **Project Manager** for a project at a client site in City, State, US operating in a fast-paced, high-energy, stimulating, challenging, and rewarding environment. The successful candidate will:

- Lead a software development team comprised of X Company Software employees
- Manage integrated project teams and initiatives comprised of resources from multiple companies
- Manage multiple project initiatives at once, and maintain flexibility to adjust priorities according to client needs
- Demonstrate understanding of full SDLC
- Have working knowledge of various project management methodologies
- Have working knowledge of project management tools (Microsoft Project, SharePoint, Project Server, HP Quality Center, etc.)
- Interface with client on a daily and continuous basis
- Exercise judgment and diplomacy working with the client, customer, team personnel, and personnel from other entities
- Maintain a polished, professional deportment while representing the company to the client, and while representing the client to other project stakeholders
- Function as a genuine leader for company personnel, providing solid direction, encouragement, coaching, discipline, and at times a lifeline
- Function as a tether between project team and corporate headquarters, maintaining a candid, open, ongoing discussion of project disposition with executive management
- Provide daily project updates as well as weekly status reports
- Conduct team personnel performance reviews and manage a salary budget pool

Position requirements:
Minimum 5 years of experience performing full-time project management and project team leadership; Minimum 10 years overall professional experience; Project management of software development teams highly preferred, but not required; Current PMP credential (or able to obtain it within 6 months) Agile and/or ITIL certifications helpful, but not required

OPERATION: CIVILIAN RÉSUMÉ

Bruce Benedict, MBA, PMP
(Major/O-4, US Army, Retired)

Address
Address
(XXX) 207-2716
Bruce@BattlefieldRésumés.com

HIGHLIGHTS OF QUALIFICATIONS

TS/SCI (Feb 2013), CI SCOPE POLYGRAPH (2008), MBA, PMP (2009)
Skilled <u>Senior Project Manager</u> *with strong proficiency and experience in the following:*

- ITIL v3 Expert
- Integrated Project Teams
- 29 yrs Project Management
- 29 yrs Project Team Leadership
- Budget Management
- Software Life Cycle Development
- Project Management Methodologies
- MS Project, Project, Server and Excel

PROFESSIONAL EXPERIENCE

Project Manager, Integrated Schedule Manager   Mar 11 - May 13
Organization, City, State
- Used Microsoft (MS) Project to track 6 concurrent, major system development programs, containing 1000 – 2500 tasks. Data from these programs were placed into an overall Integrated Master Schedule (IMS).
- Prepared detailed change reports for each integrated schedule, validating predicted milestone dates through critical path analysis of development through installation.
- Briefed customer on potential resource and personnel schedule conflicts among several concurrent system development and installation efforts, including ad hoc analyses and reports to include forecasts.
- Identifying a previously unknown development problem with a circuit card in the integrated master schedule data, revealing a retest not identified by the developer.

Project Manager, Budget / Financial Management   Nov 08 - Mar 11
Organization, City, State
- Researched and drafted the response to a Congressional inquiry about the agency's IT budget, draft comments had minimal changes prior to release to Congress.
- Facilitated the Office of Management and Budget's (OMB) requirement to review and evaluate IT spending across the Federal Government, ensured information for several agencies was correct in the Federal IT Investment Portfolio, which is part of the President's Budget.
- Identified discrepancies and drafted critical corrections for the annual Enterprise Roadmap submission to OMB, information technology summary data within the Agency IT Investment Portfolio (Exhibit 53) and the IT Capital Asset Summary (Exhibit 300). Multiple high-level reports were reconciled.
- Conducted Alternative Analysis, Benefit-Cost Analysis, the Business Reference Model (BRM) and Service Reference Model (SRM) of the Federal Enterprise Architecture (FEA) for agency-level reviews of planned initiatives that were part of a Budget Estimate Submission (BES).

Project Manager May 04 - Nov 08
Organization, City, State
- Customer witness for hardware and software integration testing at the factory and at operational locations, addressing specific areas of concern to program COTR.
- Site manager recognized the verification method used as innovative and for helping to keep a six-month network installation on schedule
- Coordinated the review of test plans, test procedures and reports that facilitated timely Government responses with little exception.
- Test witness also for a major post-installation, multi-system test and tracked requirement verification for customer test lead. Work received recognition by senior managers.
- Reduced program risk by developing a Microsoft Access database and procedures to use with the Requirements Traceability Management (RTM) tool, auditing approx. 3300 system requirements

Project Manager, Contract / CDRL Management May 03 – May 04
Organization, City, State
- Prepared Basis of Estimates (BOE) that provided several thousand labor hours and other direct costs for a successful classified program proposal, receiving a performance award for this successful effort.
- Coordinated the review, provided feedback to the customer to the Government and kept the status of several hundred Contract Data Requirements List (CDRL) submittals
- Analyzed and identified CDRLs that had outdated information or CDRLs that provided redundant information. These CDRLs were removed from the follow-on contract saving about $50,000 each.
- Assisted contracting officer in executing the withdrawal of out-dated CDRL submittals.

Project Manager, Portfolio Management Aug 98 – Mar 03
Organization, City, State
- Briefed Assistant Director to the CIO on the results of an IT portfolio benchmark analysis and the results of a market surveys for commercially available portfolio management tools - all recommendations accepted
- Defined semi-annual portfolio management process to manage the portfolio of several business IT systems, synchronizing the process to the annual Planning, Programming and Budget System (PPBS) cycle.
- Researched technical merits and cost of individual projects using business cases that were based on the Exhibit 300. Provided recommendations to the senior managers of the Investment Review Board for IT.
- Prepared 3 Congressionally-mandated semi-annual reports that provided the status of a business transformation program of record to four standing Congressional committees.

OPERATION: CIVILIAN RÉSUMÉ

EDUCATION

MBA – (school, location)	1992
BS in Organizational Behavior – (school, location)	1986

TRAINING

Program Management Office Course	2004
DoD Acquisition Courses	1989

CERTIFICATIONS

Information Technology Infrastructure Library (ITIL) v3 Expert	2013
Project Management Professional (PMP), **Program Management Institute**	2003

PRACTICE 2 (ANSWER SHEET)

Practice Vacancy 2 (Answer)

Counter Terrorism Analyst

Description:

The Mission Support Business Unit has a career opportunity for a CT/AT/FP Analyst at City, State, US. This position will provide focus for analytical efforts for regional and transnational terrorist and insurgent organizations; conduct threat assessments and vulnerability assessments of critical infrastructure pertaining to specific, potential threats in the Pacific Command (PACOM) Area of Responsibility (AOR); construct and deliver daily and weekly briefings, provide all-source analysis, conduct research, and author papers as requested to support the Command regarding issues relevant to the security of the United States and forces within the PACOM AOR as requested by the Government staff or contractor site lead; provide Counter-Terrorism (CT) threat assessments, travel briefings, and force protection support to deploying units, groups, and individuals who are traveling to various countries on leave, exercise-support, or real-world missions and provide the Command with a daily update of deployed personnel and projected deployment dates of all personnel; maintain and update the CT assessments and briefs on the G2 Operations travel briefs website/portal which will include the country threat, cultural awareness issues, and travel precautions and best practices; provide input to the Commanding General's daily read book and associated briefings; assist the G2 with organizing and providing subject matter expertise to the Threat Working Group and the Anti-Terrorism Working Group meetings and maintain situational awareness of political, economic, diplomatic, criminal, military, and terrorism-related developments; and provide exercise support, perform periodic shift work and to travel within the PACOM AOR and other CONUS locations.

Qualifications:

A Bachelor's degree in Liberal Arts/Sciences (or related field) and/or equivalent formal military training and 6 years related experience including work in all-source analysis environments with emphasis on CT, CI, AT and FP. An additional 4 years of related work experience may be considered in lieu of the Bachelor's degree. Must have a thorough understanding of the U.S. Intelligence Community, the intelligence cycle, processes and organizations as they relate to counter terrorism analysis.

Desired Qualifications

Prior experience in CT/CI/FP/AT analysis of terrorist and insurgent organizations in the PACOM area of responsibility.

Job Posting: Feb 15, 2013, 8:28:22 AM

Practice Résumé 2 (Answer)

Bruce Benedict
(SFC/E7, US Army, Retired)

Address (XXX) 207-2716
Address Bruce@BattlefieldRésumés.com

HIGHLIGHTS OF QUALIFICATIONS

TOP SECRET/SCI (2011), **MASTER'S DEGREE** in Intelligence Studies
Skilled **CT/AT/FP Analyst** *with strong experience and proficiency in the following:*

- CT/AT/FP Analysis
- Threat Assessments
- Vulnerability Assessments
- Critical Infrastructure
- All-Source Analyst
- Travel Briefings
- PACOM AOR
- Exercise Support

PROFESSIONAL EXPERIENCE

CT/AT/FP Senior Intelligence Analyst　　　　　　　　Nov 10 - Jan 13
Organization, City, State

- Reviewed and produced all-source Counterterrorism, Anti-terrorism, Force Protection (CT/AT/FP) intelligence products within the division of six personnel; provided critical intelligence assessments of developing threats to the base to ensure U.S. and local security units were able to accurately determine appropriate force protection postures during real-world and exercise scenarios.
- Formulated 3 base vulnerability assessments utilizing geospatial intelligence systems, human intelligence and counterintelligence (CI) reporting; provided approximately 15 page operational base assessments identifying physical structure, criminal, and terrorist vulnerabilities for base commanders and force protection forces to address strategies for mitigating base threats.
- Conducted threat and vulnerability assessments on regional and transnational terrorist organizations supporting Air Force in providing CT threat assessments of possible extremist groups residing in the PACOM AOR and review of intelligence information reports (IIRs); ensured case officers had the tailored intelligence to support counterintelligence operations.

CT/AT/FP Intelligence Superintendent　　　　　　　　Sep 07 - Nov 10
Organization, City, State

- Conducted pre-travel briefings for personnel traveling throughout the PACOM AOR; identified political, economic, diplomatic, criminal, military and terrorism-related developments to travelers and deployers; ensured FP package time line and security requirements for compliance with PACOM AT/FP travel program were met--no personnel loss or incidents.
- Integrated intelligence operations to produce CT/AT/FP threat assessments and intelligence participation in special Threat Working Groups.

- Received "Excellent" ratings for Inspector General compliance and operational readiness inspections for its operations in research, coordination with local and federal security teams, medical units, and foreign security teams.
- Provided force protection recommendations to unit commanders and deployed teams within the PACOM AOR.
- Oversaw the development of intelligence support to force protection operations IAW policies and regulations to support the group's real-world deployments and exercise scenarios.
- Ensure timely CT/AT/FP strategy and response planning for 758-manned unit by monitoring and reporting threat situations to the commander, staff, and deployed personnel regarding critical political, military, and terrorism related issues and capabilities to; provided daily situational updates on PACOM AOR and its operational impacts on deployed assets.

Sr. All-Source Analyst Jul 04 - Sep 07
Organization, City, State
- Oversaw the production of intelligence to identify illicit trafficking, internal security measures, threat networks and key personalities involved in narcotics production, trafficking, and related criminal and terrorism financing or operations to support theater- and national-level counternarcotics and CT missions.
- Applied advanced intelligence collection and production concepts, principles, practices, laws, regulations, methods, and techniques to provide counter narco-terrorism intelligence products for U.S. and host-nation counternarcotics and CT forces.
- Supervised and managed the division of 6 personnel leading all-source collection management and intelligence operations team providing collection requirements management and HUMINT and IMINT production, interpretation, analysis, and dissemination of national intelligence products in support of counterdrug assessments and operations.

Collection Manager, HUMINT Dec 02 - Jul 04
Organization, City, State
- Authored, prioritized, and validated standing (long-term) and ad hoc (short-term) HUMINT collection requirements to joint, national, theater, and organic collections assets in support of COCOM Priority Intelligence Requirements and AT/FP requirements.

Indications & Warning (I&W) Analyst Apr 01 - Dec 02
Organization, City, State
- Conducted CT and AT/FP intelligence warning and assessments to commanders and deployed personnel to ensure commanders were able to execute appropriate FP postures to protect personnel and assets.

- Ensured the timely I&W support of over 9000 airlift and sealift missions in support of Operations Enduring Freedom by reviewing and managing the screening of over 2000 messages per day and providing relevant AT/FP intelligence to command planners and operators.
- I&W Watch Shift NCOIC: led fused multi-source reporting on existing or pending military and terrorism threats to the COCOM and component personnel and assets operating worldwide.

EDUCATION

MA, Intelligence Studies (school, location)	2013
BS, Management/Human Resources, (school, location)	2003
AA, General Studies, (school, location)	2001
AAS, Communications Applications Technology, (school, location)	2000
AAS, Logistics, (school, location)	1998

TRAINING

CI Missions and Functions	2011
Enlisted Intelligence Master Skills	2010
Strategic Debriefing of Law Enforcement Sources	2007
J2X (CI/HUMINT) Operations Course	2007
Joint Collection Management	2006
Intelligence, Surveillance, & Reconnaissance Fundamentals	2005
Intelligence Collection Course	2005
Intelligence Support to Force Protection	2005
Joint Combined Interagency Intelligence	2004
Warning Analysis	2002
Joint Intelligence Analyst Course	2001
All-Source Analyst Course	1996

PRACTICE 3 (ANSWER SHEET)

Practice Vacancy 3 (Answer)

Our computer forensics professionals analyze digital media and evidence providing detailed analysis to help uncover essential facts and insights. We can bring to bear the range of our forensic investigation skill set to help our clients with their investigations. We have developed methodologies and strategies that help clients handle difficult circumstances.

Description:
- Function as investigative resource; provide technical expertise while also learning the use of utilizing cutting edge tools and techniques to extract, analyze and report on captured data
- Perform accurate analysis and effective diagnosis of client issues and manage day-to-day client relationships at peer client levels.
- Assist in proposal development, as requested.

Required Skills:
- Minimum of 5 years of experience industry experience
- Ability to work independently and manage multiple task assignments
- Demonstrated expertise in computer forensics
- Willingness to travel both within the U.S. and internationally per client needs
- Bachelor's degree from an accredited four-year institution
- Expertise with the Microsoft operating system internals (e.g., registry, file formats, common artifact locations)
- Demonstrated knowledge of industry-standard computer forensics software and hardware
- Willingness to work in criminal investigations and provide expert testimony
· Secret security clearance

Preferred Skills:
· Moderate oral and written communication skills, including presentation skills (MS Visio, MS PowerPoint)
· Proficiency with Microsoft Excel and Word
· Problem solving and troubleshooting skills with the ability to exercise mature judgment
· Experience in criminal investigations
· Industry certifications, including CFCE, CCE, EnCE, ACE, GCFA, GCFE.
· Expertise with non-Microsoft operating systems (e.g., OS X, Linux, iOS, Android)

Practice Résumé 3 (Answer)

Bruce Benedict
MBA, PMP, CISSP

(XXX) 207-2716   Bruce@BattlefieldRésumé.com

HIGHLIGHTS OF QUALIFICATIONS

TOP SECRET (2009), MBA & MS in Information Systems
Skilled <u>Computer Forensics Professional</u> *with strong experience in the following:*

- Encase, FTK, Paraben
- CHFI, EC_ECSA (Projected 2013)
- CISSP, CEH, MCSE, Net+, CCNA
- Nessus, eRetina, AppDetective, PGP,SRR

- Investigations
- NIST SP 800 series
- SAP, Oracle
- MCT, CTT

PROFESSIONAL EXPERIENCE

Sr. Cyber Information Systems Auditor   **Dec 12 - Apr 13**
Organization, City, State
➢ Scrutinizes digital evidence within Symantec Endpoint. Created a logical image with FTK to gain an understanding of the evidence.
➢ Discovered normal files, returned deleted files to their original state.
➢ Crafted five NIST 800 53 Series policies including Incident Response Policies and Procedures, Responds to and investigates potential incidents to rule out false positives, validate and search for forensic evidence. Created logical images with FTK and determined false positive.
➢ Performs gap analysis for the Department's GSS and NIST 800-53A Rev 3 series of 17 families of controls. Recommended a patch policy.

Sr. Cyber Security Consultant   **Dec 11 - Dec 12**
Organization, City, State
➢ Consulted on forensic reports and all security issues with CIO's and CEOs of other Cyber Security SBA organizations.
➢ Evaluated and analyzed the security profile of the CMS network infrastructure in relationship to the NIST 800-53A Rev 3 control family, including the output of the vulnerability scans. The results provided a recommendation for the Authority to Operate for the system.
➢ Served as a Cyber-Security and technical Subject Matter Expert for all related security investigations.
➢ Managed relationships with federal partners. Briefed trends to DoD and federal government officials and corporate executives.

Sr. Cyber Security and Privacy Consultation   **Nov 09 - Dec 11**
Organization, City, State
➢ Extracted, analyzed and presented complex web application vulnerabilities,

- including Cross Site Scripting and SQL injections for applications in the development for the Department.
- Detected potential attack vectors, by identifying persistent cookies with user names embedded in them.
- Developed process of implementing non-forensically acceptable tools to expedite an Encase investigation.
- Analyzed the Medicare Network through interviewing four different groups of key stakeholders and evaluating technical, operational and management controls.
- Led the team with approximately 14 people in the resolution of Project Objectives and Milestones for GSS.
- Analyzed client's security issues on the Medicare contract.

Sr. Cyber Information System Security Engineer, Manager   Jan 08 - Nov 09
Organization, City, State
- Analyzed detailed results of an audit, and led a team of 10 people in the resolution of over 650 findings for the eVerify Information System leading to an ATO and 13 Project Objectives and Milestones.
- Created and implemented a plan for network security architecture for delivery of a private cloud infrastructure to federal clients.
- Created Statement of Work for multiple contracts.

Sr Cyber Security Engineer   Jul 07 - Jan 08
Organization, City, State
- Conducted vulnerability assessment testing and implemented tools for the Certification and Accreditation (C & A) package on assigned Military Health System sites utilizing DITSCAP & DIACAP guidelines. These included networks which required a CAC card.
- Conducted automated vulnerability scans using Retina Network Scanner, App Detective, and Production Gold Disks, security checklists and scripts for UNIX and Oracle 10g. The tests and interviews verified or identified deviations from the DoD requirements for the applicable Military Health System.
- Created and presented Reports and POA&Ms to the DAA

Cyber Quality Control Consultant   Dec 06 – Jul 07
Organization, City, State
- Conducted access control testing to insure appropriate permissions were in place as it related to financial applications supporting Federal Student Aid Loan processing; these included applications utilizing Java, C and C++.
- Monitored initiation, development, tests and implementation of software development lifecycle to identify and track risks qualitatively, and provided recommendations on corrective and preventative actions.
- Analyzed and reviewed requirements and security plans for Federal Student Aid GSS.
- Conducted Security Tests and Evaluation testing for major applications released into production.

OPERATION: CIVILIAN RÉSUMÉ

CISCO Project Lead   Sep 01 - Dec 06
Organization, City, State
- Established a successful CISCO curriculum.
- Instructed the MCSE courses leading students to an MCSE certification.

Microsoft Sr. Systems Engineer   Feb 01 – Jun 01
Organization, City, State
- Operated and managed the MS Exchange and MS Windows servers for DoD.
- Analyzed and recommended updates for UPS system, Evaluated and crafted Disaster Recovery plan and procedures. Participated in the creation of the SSAA and the System Security Plan.
- Managed day-to-day client activities.

EDUCATION

MBA, Finance	(school, location)	2005
MS, Information Systems	(school, location)	2000
BS, Biology	(school, location)	1998

TRAINING / CERTIFICATIONS

- CISSP
- CISM
- CEH
- MCSE
- MCT
- CTT
- Unix
- Net+
- CCNA
- Encase
- FTK
- Oracle
- Windows
- Paraben
- Nessus
- NMAP
- eRetina
- AppDetective
- NTO Spider
- Production Gold Disk
- SRR
- Symantic Endpoint
- Websense
- SAP

PRACTICE 4 (ANSWER SHEET)

Practice Vacancy 4 (Answer)

Cyber Counterintelligence Analyst Job, Date: Apr 17, 2013
Location: City, State, US
Description: Serve as a counterintelligence (CI) specialist and provide subject matter expertise to IC members fulfilling their CI responsibilities. Respond to cyber-related CI, Information Assurance (IA), and security incidents and conduct computer forensic analysis of hardware, firmware, and software. Run forensic examinations and analysis on systems, networks, and digital multimedia as directed by the client and draft written reports. Apply knowledge and mastery of CI concepts, principles, and practices to plan and conduct a full range of CI support to operations, investigations, analysis, and CI services. Employ knowledge of CI functional areas and state-of-the-art technologies, analytical tools, and communications processes to act independently to support CI activities. Develop analytical processes and methods to support cyber CI investigations and CI analysis and production. Exercise knowledge of the appropriate directives, regulations, policies, and procedures necessary to independently perform and supervise technical and administrative CI functions. Liaise with senior members and staff of the supported agency and leadership and staff throughout the CI and law enforcement communities.

Basic Qualifications: 5+ years of experience as a credentialed special agent-5+ years of experience with intelligence analysis, including counterintelligence, counterterrorism, cyber, cyber security, computer forensics, and law enforcement missions-5+ years of experience with offensive CI operations or CI investigations-5+ years of experience with CI, LE, Cyber Security, computer forensics-5+ years of experience with intelligence community roles, responsibilities, organizations, and capabilities-TS/SCI clearance required-BA or BS degree **required**

Additional Qualifications: Experience with Palantir, Analyst Notebook, HOTR, M3, or similar network analysis and message dissemination systems-Knowledge of the organizations and functions of the DoD CI and HUMINT community-Knowledge of the Missile Defense Agency (MDA) and the Ballistic Missile Defense System (BMDS)-Knowledge of DoD 5240.21, DoD Instruction 5240.26, DoD Instruction 5240.23, US Public Law, and DoD intelligence oversight policy issuances-Knowledge of the structure, policies, and directives of national intelligence agencies and organizations-Ability to interact with military and civilian senior representatives of national intelligence agencies-Possession of excellent oral and written communication skills-Computer Forensics Certifications, including EnCase or Access Data FTK (Forensic Tool Kit)

Clearance: Applicants selected will be subject to a security investigation and may need to meet eligibility requirements for access to classified information; TS/SCI clearance is required.

Practice Résumé 4 (Answer)

Bruce Benedict

(XXX) 207-2716 Bruce@BattlefieldRésumés.com

HIGHLIGHTS OF QUALIFICATIONS

TS/SCI (2012), CI SCOPE POLYGRAPH (2009), MS Degree, CI Agent
Skilled **Cyber CI Special Agent** *with strong experience in the following:*

- Cyber Forensics SME
- CI/CT/LE Cyber Analysis
- Network incident response
- ASOC, MCC Collection
- CI Investigations
- Certified Ethical Hacker
- Certified Forensic Examiner
- Operating System/Network Analysis
- Wireshark, Snort, Encase, and FTK
- Forensics/Intrusion Analysis

PROFESSIONAL EXPERIENCE

Cyber Counterintelligence (CI) Special Agent   **Jul 09 - Present**
Organization, City, State
- Operates as a Subject Matter Expert (SME) in multiple capacities performing Enterprise-level cyber security operations, insider threat detection and investigation, cyber forensics, cyber threat analysis and cyber intelligence IAW DoDI S-5240.23.
- Conducts forensic analysis of classified and unclassified network computer systems pertaining to policy violations and network intrusions.
- Conducts and manages full scope Cyber CI investigations in addition to incident response, digital collections and examinations (dead box, live, mobile and network).
- Responds to Cyber incidents, including insider threat and network intrusions that involve Army computers in area of responsibility.

Cyber Intelligence Specialist-Operations   **Jun 02 - Jul 09**
Organization, City, State
- Cyber Subject Matter Expert (SME) in multiple capacities managing a BMDS Cyber security project covering security events, tools and techniques.
- Represented the organization at national-level US Government Joint Task Force cyber threat working groups as the resident subject matter expert.
- Planned, coordinated, and executed cyber collection operations utilizing best methodology while adhering to local and national-level operational and oversight guidelines.
- Liaised with cyber security personnel from public, private, and government sectors at cyber security conferences in North America, Europe, and Asia.
- Conducted targeted analysis on hacking, hacking tools, and hacking TTPs, which resulted in numerous information reports for network security community.

Technology Coordinator	Jun 02 - Jun 06
Organization, City, State
- Supervised division-level technology help desk personnel, network engineer/technology administrator.
- Managed user network shares and user accounts in active directory for a division of 1000 plus users.
- Collaborated with twelve regional technology directors from Hewlett Packard, Microsoft, and Sun Software to create Instructional Technology (IT) curriculum that was accepted and implemented for 4 divisions consisting of 3,800 students and 384 staff.
- Led complex change, approving technology budgets, managing and updating technology equipment, and training end users on numerous hardware and software.
- Taught graduate-level technology coursework on technology integration to on-site Masters cohort consisting of over 36 adult learners through the State's University system.

Technology Coordinator/Educator	Jun 99 - Jun 02
Organization, City, State
- Led technology integration into a school system such as managing technology budget, purchasing technology hardware and software, and teaching technology courses
- Managed network shares and user accounts on Windows 2000 network
- Served as school webmaster responsible for creating and maintaining website as well as providing website development courses to teaching and administrative staff
- Presented Technology Integration at an international Conference on Technology
- Trained over 40 staff members on hardware and software including: Microsoft products, Blackboard, Adobe, and Video Editing Software

EDUCATION

MS in Digital Forensic Science, (school, location)	2014
MA in Leadership Studies & Educational Technology, (school, location)	2001
MS in Teaching Credential, (school, location)	1997
BA in International Relations, (school, location)	1993

TRAINING

Technical Training

Certified Ethical Hacker Training (CEH) V8, EC-Council	2013
Access Data Mobile Phone Examiner (MPE+)	2012
Encase 7 Basic Course	2012
Encase 7 Intermediate Course	2012
SANS 408 – Computer Forensic Investigations, Windows In-Depth	2012
FIWE-Forensics & Intrusions in Windows Environment	2011
WFE-Windows Forensics – Encase	2011
OUT-Online Undercover Techniques	2011
MCCU-Managing Computer Crime Units	2010
CAC-Cyber Analyst Course	2010
Introduction to Cyber Investigations	2010
CIRC-Computer Incident Response Course	2009
INCH-Introduction to Networks and Computers	2009
WetStone - Hacking Boot camp for Investigators	2008
Network Security + Course	2008
Certified Ethical Hacker Training (CEH) V5, EC-Council	2008
International Penetration Tester Training (IPT)	2008
Cyber Investigations Training, Computer Search and Seizure	2007
Managing and Maintaining a Microsoft Windows 2003 Server	2005
Creating websites with ASP.Net 2.0 with Visual Studio	2005

Military Intelligence Training

Military Counterintelligence Collection (MCC)	2010
Advanced Source Operations Course (ASOC)	2010
Strategic Debriefing Course (DSDC)	2007
Chinese Mandarin Course, Defense Language Institute (DLI)	1990
Counterintelligence Special Agent Course (CISAC)	1990

CERTIFICATIONS

Certified Ethical Hacker (CEH)	2013
GIAC/SANS Certified Forensic Examiner (GCFE)	2012
DOD Cyber Crime Investigator	2011
DOD Forensic Examiner	2011
DOD Digital Media Collector	2010

APPENDIX B (ACTION VERBS)

Action Verbs

A
abated
abbreviated
abolished
abridged
absolved
absorbed
accelerated
accentuated
accommodated
accomplished
accounted for
accrued
accumulated
achieved
acquired
acted
adapted
adopted
added
addressed
adjusted
administered
advanced
advertised
advised
advocated
affirmed
aided
alerted
aligned
allayed
alleviated
allocated
allotted
altered
amassed
amended
analyzed
answered
anticipated
appeased
applied
appointed
appraised
approached
appropriated
approved
arbitrated
aroused
arranged
articulated
ascertained
aspired
assembled
assessed
assigned
assimilated
assisted
assured
attained
attended
audited
augmented
authored
authorized
automated
averted
avoided
awarded

B
balanced
began
benchmarked
benefited
bid
billed
blended
blocked
bolstered
boosted
bought
branded
bridged
broadened
brought
budgeted
built

C
calculated
calibrated
capitalized
captured
cared for
carried
carved
categorized
catalogued
caught
cautioned
cemented
certified
chaired
challenged
championed

changed
charged
charted
checked
chose
chronicled
circulated
circumvented
cited
clarified
classified
cleaned
cleared
closed
coached
coded
collaborated
collated
collected
combined
commanded
commended
commenced
commissioned
communicated
compared
compiled
complemented
completed
complied
composed
compounded
computed
conceived
concentrated
conceptualized
condensed

conducted
conferred
configured
confirmed
confronted
connected
conserved
considered
consolidated
constructed
consulted
consummated
contacted
continued
contracted
contributed
controlled
converted
conveyed
convinced
cooperated
coordinated
copied
corrected
corresponded
counseled
created
critiqued
cultivated
customized
cut

D
dealt
debated
debugged

decided
decoded
decreased
dedicated
defined
delegated
delineated
delivered
demonstrated
deployed
derived
described
designated
designed
detailed
detected
determined
developed
devised
diagnosed
differentiated
diffused
directed
disbursed
discovered
discussed
dispatched
dispensed
displayed
disposed
disproved
dissected
disseminated
dissolved
distinguished
distributed

diversified
diverted
divested
divided
documented
doubled
drafted
dramatized
drew up
drove

E
earned
eased
economized
edited
educated
effected
elaborated
elected
elevated
elicited
eliminated
embraced
emphasized
empowered
enabled
encouraged
ended
enforced
engaged
engineered
enhanced
enlisted
enriched
enrolled

ensured
entered
entertained
enticed
equipped
established
estimated
evaluated
examined
exceeded
executed
exercised
exhibited
expanded
expedited
experienced
experimented
explained
explored
expressed
extended
extracted

F
fabricated
facilitated
factored
familiarized
fashioned
fielded
filed
filled
finalized
financed
fine tuned
finished

fixed
focused
followed
forecasted
forged
formalized
formed
formulated
fortified
forwarded
fostered
fought
found
founded
framed
fulfilled
functioned as
funded
furnished
furthered

G
gained
garnered
gathered
gauged
gave
generated
governed
graduated
grasped
greeted
grew
grouped
guaranteed
guided

H
halted
halved
handled
headed
heightened
held
helped
hired
honed
hosted
hypnotized
hypothesized

I
identified
ignited
illustrated
implemented
imported
improved
improvised
incited
included
incorporated
increased
indicated
individualized
indoctrinated
induced
influenced
informed
infused
initiated
innovated
inspected

inspired
installed
instilled
instituted
instructed
insured
integrated
intensified
interacted
interceded
interpreted
intervened
interviewed

invented
inventoried
invested
investigated
invigorated
invited
involved
isolated
issued
itemized

J
joined
judged
justified

L
launched
learned
lectured
led
lessened
leveraged

licensed
lifted
limited
linked
liquidated
listened
litigated
loaded
located
logged

M
made
maintained
managed
mandated
maneuvered
manipulated
manufactured
mapped
marked
marketed
mastered
maximized
measured
mediated
memorized
mentored
merged
merited
met
minimized
mobilized
modeled
moderated
modified

molded
monitored
monopolized
motivated
mounted
moved
multiplied

N
named
narrated
navigated
negotiated
netted
neutralized
nominated
normalized
notified
nurtured

O
observed
obtained
offered
officiated
offset
opened
operated
optimized
orchestrated
ordered
organized
oriented
originated
outdistanced
outlined

outperformed
overcame
overhauled
oversaw
owned

P
paced
packaged
packed
pared
participated
partnered
passed
penetrated
perceived
perfected
performed
persuaded
photographed
piloted
pinpointed
pioneered
placed
planned
played
praised
predicted
prepared
prescribed
presented
preserved
presided
prevailed
prevented
printed
prioritized

processed
procured
produced
profiled
programmed
progressed
projected
promoted
proofread
proposed
protected
proved
provided
pruned
publicized
purchased
pursued

Q
quadrupled
qualified
quantified
queried
questioned
quoted

R
raised
rallied
ranked
rated
reached
read
realigned
realized

rearranged
reasoned
rebuilt
received
recognized
recommended
reconciled
reconstructed
recorded
recovered
recruited
rectified
redesigned
redirected
reduced
re-engineered
referred
refocused
registered
regulated

rehabilitated
reinforced
reiterated
related
released
relied
relieved
remained
remodeled
rendered
renegotiated
renewed
reorganized
repaired
replaced
replied

replicated
reported
represented
reproduced
requested
researched
reserved
resolved
responded
restored
restructured
retained
retooled
retrieved
returned
revamped
reversed
reviewed
revised
revitalized
revolutionized
rewarded
risked
rotated
routed

S
safeguarded
salvaged
saved
scanned
scheduled
screened
sculptured
searched
secured

seized
selected
sent
separated
sequenced
served
serviced
set up
settled
shaped
shared
sharpened
shipped
shortened
showed
signed
simplified
simulated
sketched
slashed
smoothed
solicited
sold
solidified
solved
sorted
sourced
sparked
spearheaded
specialized
specified
speculated
spent
spoke
sponsored
spurred
staffed

standardized
started
steered
stimulated
streamlined
strengthened
stretched
structured
studied
submitted
succeeded
suggested
summarized
supervised
supplied
supported
surpassed
surveyed
swayed
swept
symbolized
synthesized
systemized

T
tabulated
tackled
talked
tallied
targeted
tasted
taught
teamed

tempered
tended
terminated
tested
testified
tied
took
topped
totaled
traced
tracked
trained
transcribed
transformed
transitioned
translated
transmitted
traveled
treated
trimmed
tripled
troubleshot
turned
tutored
typed

U
uncovered
underlined
underscored
undertook
underwrote
unearthed

unified
united
updated
upgraded
upheld
urged
used
utilized

V
validated
valued
vaulted
verbalized
verified
viewed
visualized
voiced
volunteered

W
weathered
weighed
widened
withstood
won
worked
wove
wrote

Y
yielded

APPENDIX C
(TARGETED VERBS)

Management/Leadership Skills

administered
analyzed
appointed
approved
assigned
attained
authorized
chaired
considered
consolidated
contracted
controlled
converted
coordinated
decided
delegated
developed
directed
eliminated
emphasized
enforced
enhanced
established
executed
generated
handled
headed
hired
hosted
improved
incorporated
increased
initiated
inspected
instituted
led
managed
merged
motivated
organized
originated
overhauled
oversaw
planned
presided
prioritized
produced
recommended
reorganized
replaced
restored
reviewed
scheduled
streamlined
strengthened
supervised
terminated

Communication/People Skills

addressed
advertised
arbitrated
arranged
articulated
authored
clarified
collaborated
communicated
composed
condensed
conferred
consulted
contacted
conveyed
convinced
corresponded
debated
defined
described
developed
directed
discussed
drafted
edited
elicited
enlisted
explained
expressed
formulated
furnished
incorporated
influenced
interacted
interpreted
interviewed
involved
joined
judged
lectured
listened
marketed
mediated
moderated
negotiated
observed
outlined

participated
persuaded
presented
promoted
proposed
publicized
reconciled
recruited
referred
reinforced
reported
resolved
responded
solicited
specified
spoke
suggested
summarized
synthesized
translated
wrote

Research Skills
analyzed
clarified
collected
compared
conducted
critiqued
detected
determined
diagnosed
evaluated
examined
experimented
explored
extracted
formulated
gathered
identified
inspected
interpreted
interviewed
invented
investigated
located
measured
organized
researched
searched
solved
summarized
surveyed
systematized
tested

Technical Skills
adapted
assembled
built
calculated
computed
conserved
constructed
converted
debugged
designed
determined
developed
engineered
fabricated
fortified
installed
maintained
operated
overhauled
printed
programmed
rectified
regulated
remodeled
repaired
replaced
restored
solved
specialized
standardized
studied
upgraded
utilized

Teaching Skills
adapted
advised
clarified
coached
communicated
conducted
coordinated
critiqued
developed
enabled
encouraged
evaluated
explained
facilitated
focused
guided
individualized
informed
instilled

instructed
motivated
persuaded
set goals
simulated
stimulated
taught
tested
trained
transmitted
tutored

**Financial/
Data Skills**
administered
adjusted
allocated
analyzed
appraised
assessed
audited
balanced
calculated
computed
conserved
corrected
determined
developed
estimated
forecasted
managed
marketed
measured
planned
programmed
projected
reconciled

reduced
researched
retrieved
creative skills
acted
adapted
began
combined
conceptualized
condensed
created
customized
designed
developed
directed
displayed
drew
entertained
established
fashioned
formulated
founded
illustrated
initiated
instituted
integrated
introduced
invented
modeled
modified
originated
performed
photographed
planned
revised
revitalized
shaped

solved

Helping skills
adapted
advocated
aided
answered
arranged
assessed
assisted
cared for
clarified
coached
collaborated
contributed
cooperated
counseled
demonstrated
diagnosed
educated
encouraged
ensured
expedited
facilitated
familiarize
furthered
guided
helped
insured
intervened
motivated
provided
referred
rehabilitated
presented
resolved

simplified
supplied
supported
volunteered

**Organization/
Detail Skills**
approved
arranged
cataloged
categorized
charted
classified
coded
collected
compiled
corresponded
distributed
executed
filed
generated
implemented

incorporated
inspected
logged
maintained
monitored
obtained
operated
ordered
organized
prepared
processed
provided
purchased
recorded
registered
reserved
responded
reviewed
routed
scheduled
screened
set up
submitted

supplied
standardized
systematized
updated
validated
verified

**More verbs for
Accomplishments**
achieved
completed
expanded
exceeded
improved
pioneered
reduced (losses)
resolved (issues)
restored
spearheaded
succeeded
surpassed
transformed
won

APPENDIX D (COMPETENCIES)

Competencies are observable behaviors that encompass the knowledge, skills and personal characteristics that distinguish levels of performance in the work environment.

As referenced in OPM's Government wide occupational study using its *Multipurpose Occupational Systems Analysis Inventory - Close-Ended* (MOSAIC) methodology, the below are a few competencies for a wide range of human resource management functions.

A
Accountability - Holds self and others accountable for measurable high-quality, timely, and cost-effective results. Determines objectives, sets priorities, and delegates work. Accepts responsibility for mistakes.

Administration and Management - Knowledge of planning, coordination and execution of business functions, resource allocation and production.

Applies Technology to Tasks - Selects and understands procedures, machines or tools that will produce the desired results; identifies or solves problems in machines, computers, or other technologies as they are related to performing tasks.

B
Budget Administration - Knowledge of the principles and practices of budget administration and analysis; including preparing, justifying, reporting on and executing the budget; and the relationships among program, budget, accounting, and reporting systems.

C
Capacity Management - Knowledge of the principles and methods for monitoring, estimating or reporting actual performance or the performance capability of information systems or components.

Change Management - Knowledge of change management principles, strategies and techniques required for effectively planning, implementing, and evaluating change in the organization.

Clerical - Knowledge of filing, typing, entering data, maintaining records, taking shorthand, and using and completing forms.

Client Engagement/Change Management - Knowledge of the impact of change on people, processes, procedures, leadership, and organizational culture; knowledge of change management principles, strategies, and techniques required for effectively planning, implementing, and evaluating change in the organization.

Communications Security Management - Knowledge of the principles, policies and procedures involved in ensuring the security of communications services and data, and in maintaining the communications environment on which it resides.

Computer Forensics - Knowledge of tools and techniques used in data recovery and preservation of electronic evidence.

Computer Languages - Knowledge of computer languages and their applications to enable a system to perform specific functions.

Computer Network Defense - Knowledge of defensive measures to detect, responds, and protect information, information systems, and networks from threats.

Computer Skills - Uses computers, software applications, databases and automated systems to accomplish work.

Conflict Management (*) - Manages and resolves conflicts, grievances, confrontations, or disagreements in a constructive manner to minimize negative personal impact. Encourages creative tension and differences of opinions. Anticipates and takes steps to prevent counter-productive confrontations. Manages and resolves conflicts and disagreements in a constructive manner.

D
Database Administration - Knowledge of the principles, methods, and tools for automating, developing, implementing, or administering database systems.

Design - Knowledge of conceptualizing, developing, producing, understanding, and using plans, models, blueprints, and maps, including the use of tools and instruments to produce precision technical drawings, working prototypes, components, or systems.

E
Education and Training - Knowledge of teaching, training, research, making presentations, lecturing, testing and other instructional methods.

OPERATION: CIVILIAN RÉSUMÉ

Employee Development - Knowledge of employee development concepts, principles, and practices related to planning, evaluating, and administering training, organizational development, and career development initiatives.

F
Financial Analysis - Knowledge of the principles, methods, and techniques of financial analysis, forecasting, and modeling to interpret quantitative and qualitative data; includes data modeling, earned value management, and evaluating key financial indicators, trends, and historical data.

Financial Management - Understands the organization's financial processes. Prepares, justifies, and administers the program budget. Oversees procurement and contracting to achieve desired results. Monitors expenditures and uses cost-benefit thinking to set priorities.

Forensics - Knowledge of procedures of civil, criminal, or administrative hearings, evidence collection, including the delivery and receipt of evidence, classes of evidence, and rules of evidence and legal procedures.

H
Human Capital Management - Builds and manages workforce based on organizational goals, budget considerations, and staffing needs. Ensures that employees are appropriately recruited, selected, appraised, and rewarded; takes action to address performance problems. Manages a multi-sector workforce and a variety of work situations.

I
Information Assurance - Knowledge of methods and procedures to protect information systems and data by ensuring their availability, authentication, confidentiality, and integrity.

Information Management - Identifies a need for and knows where or how to gather information; organizes and maintains information or information management systems.

Information Systems/Network Security - Knowledge of methods, tools, and procedures, including development of information security plans, to prevent information systems vulnerabilities, and provide or restore security of information systems and network services.

Information Technology Architecture - Knowledge of architectural methodologies used in the design and development of information systems, including the physical structure of a system's internal operations and interactions with other systems.

Internal Controls - Knowledge of the principles, methods, and techniques for establishing internal control activities (for example, authorizations, verifications, reconciliations), monitoring their use, and evaluating their performance (for example, identification of material weaknesses or significant deficiencies).

O

Organizational Performance Analysis - Knowledge of the methods, techniques, and tools used to analyze program, organizational, and mission performance; includes methods that deliver key performance information (for example, comparative, trend, diagnostic, root cause, predictive) used to inform decisions, actions, communications, and accountability systems.

P

Personnel Security and Safety - Knowledge of methods and controls of personnel, public safety, and security operations; investigation and inspection techniques; or rules, regulations,
precautions, and prevention techniques for the protection of people, data, or property.

Planning and Evaluating - Organizes work, sets priorities, and determines resource requirements; determines short- or long-term goals and strategies to achieve them; coordinates with other organizations or parts of the organization to accomplish goals; monitors progress and evaluates outcomes.

Project Management - Knowledge of the principles, methods, or tools for developing, scheduling, coordinating, and managing projects and resources, including monitoring and inspecting costs, work, and contractor performance.

S

Stakeholder Management - Knowledge of the concepts, practices, and techniques used to identify, engage, influence, and monitor relationships with individuals and groups connected to a work effort; including those actively involved, those who exert influence over the process and its results, and those who have a vested interest in the outcome (positive or negative).

T

Technical Competence - Uses knowledge that is acquired through formal training or extensive on-the-job experience to perform one's job; works with, understands, and evaluates technical information related to the job; advises others on technical issues.

V

Vulnerabilities Assessment - Knowledge of the principles, methods and tools for assessing vulnerabilities, and developing or recommending appropriate mitigation countermeasures.

GLOSSARY

OPERATION: CIVILIAN RÉSUMÉ

"**The Battlefield**" ₜₘ: The vacancy announcement.

"**The Battle**" ₜₘ: Each vacancy announcement you apply to.

"**Operations Order/Weapon**" ₜₘ: Your résumé.

"**The Enemy/High Value Target**" ₜₘ: The person who will review your résumé against the vacancy announcement requirements. In this workbook, this person is referred to as the hiring manager, selecting official or recruiter.

"**Your Mission**" ₜₘ: to acquire/occupy the key terrain.

"**The War**" ₜₘ: The culmination of all battles.

"**Win the War**" ₜₘ: being hired for the job you applied to.

"**Other Soldiers**" ₜₘ: describes your competition or the list of other applicants applying to the same vacancy announcement.

"**Key Terrain**" ₜₘ: The invitation to be interviewed.

"**Avenue of Approach (AA)**" ₜₘ – This is the route you choose in which to maneuver through the terrain in order to achieve each objective on the battlefield. Avenues of Approaches are based on the capabilities, opportunities and critical information obtained by analyzing the area of operation (also known as the "AO"). An Avenue of Approach is depicted on the battlefield as a dotted line to each objective.

"**Area of Operations (AO)**" ₜₘ – This is the general work and skill area from which information and intelligence are required to permit planning of your successful operation. An example of an Area of Operation is a career area, such as the intelligence career field or the medical career field. The Area of Operation usually consists of multiple vacancies for the same type of position. For example, if you were looking at an Intelligence Analyst vacancy announcement, then the Area of Interest (AI) would be the use of multiple Intelligence Analyst vacancy announcements. Another example would be a Registered Respiratory Therapist vacancy announcement within the medical career field. The Area of Operation includes vacancy announcements from multiple companies and/or organizations that will help in identifying patterns, key words and vacancy requirements.

"Course of Action (COA)" ᴛᴍ – This is the tailored strategy, theme or format that you choose based on intelligence gathered from your Area of Operation. Your Course of Action should offer you the best chance of success in achieving your mission.

"Decision Point (DP)" ᴛᴍ - The point where you must anticipate making a decision concerning a specific Course of Action. Decision Points are usually associated with vacancy requirements.

"Direction of Attack" ᴛᴍ - A specific direction that the main attack or the main body of the force will follow. The Direction of Attack is depicted on a map as shown below. An example of this is when a hiring manager writes a

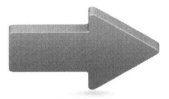

vacancy announcement, often times they will start from the top and describe the position needing filled, then move their way down the page to the applicant requirements for the position. However, as the applicant, your direction of attack should be from the bottom of the vacancy upward. This ensures that you read the vacancy requirements first to confirm you are qualified for the position prior to applying for it (or otherwise known as entering into battle).

"Enemy/High Value Target (HVT)" ₜₘ – This is the hiring manager and/or Selecting Official who wrote the vacancy announcement and/or who will read your résumé to determine if you deserve an interview. The High Value Target is shown below as a red circle with an X through the middle.

"Indicator" ₜₘ – An indicator is the evidence of an activity or any characteristic of the Area of Operation that points toward the hiring manager's desired applicant/employee experience. These indicators may influence the hiring manager's selection decision. For example, if an action verb is mentioned repetitively, this is an indicator that the hiring manager wants to see this term in your résumé to describe your work experiences.

"Key Terrain" ₜₘ - This is the area of ground on the battlefield that provides all participants an advantage in battle. Key terrain is often selected for use as objectives.

"Objective" ₜₘ – These are critical points/locations on the battlefield that must be reached and accomplished in order to move to the next phase of the operation. The objective symbol is shown below:

"Pattern Analysis" ₜₘ – This is when you analyze key terminology and vacancy announcement descriptions and evaluate patterns in the Area of Operation. Pattern analysis leads to the development of your tailored Course of Action strategy.

"Phase Lines (PL)" ₜₘ – A line used for control and coordination of military operations. It is usually a recognizable feature. Phase Lines are normally used to synchronize timing of operations. In this workbook, phase lines are associated with each of the five Intelligence Preparation of the Battlefield factors.

"Requirement" ₜₘ – These are the required skill areas needed to apply to a vacancy announcement. In other words, these are the required skills needed in order to enter into battle.

"Weapon" ₜₘ – Your weapon is your résumé. A tailored résumé is like a precisely calibrated weapon that will accurately hit a specific target 99% of the time.

INDEX

A

AA, 9, 16, 52, 55, 58, 61, 65, 67, 68, 70, 142
Analyze, v, 16, 26, 29, 31, 33, 35, 36, 37, 40, 43, 46, 47, 96
AO, 9, 10, 11, 15, 142, 143, 144
Area of Interest, 9, 142
Area of Operation, 9, 42, 142
Avenue of Approach, 9, 13, 60, 61, 142
Awards, 22

B

Battle, 6, 44, 52, 55, 58, 65, 70, 142
Battlefield, v, 5, 6, 8, 9, 13, 15, 26, 142

C

Certification, 23
COA, 10, 11, 143, 144
Course of Action, 10, 143

D

Decision Point, 10, 143
Defense Department, 1, 7
Department of Defense, 63
Describe, v, 16, 18
Direction of Attack, 10, 143
DP, 10, 143

E

Education, 29, 31, 33, 35, 37, 40
Enemy, v, 6, 10, 15, 60, 61, 142, 143
Evaluate, v, 16, 42, 43, 45

F

Federal Government, 3, 149
Format, 51

H

High Value Target, 6, 10, 142, 143
HIGHLIGHTS OF QUALIFICATIONS, 75, 81, 87, 93, 103, 108, 99, 118
Hiring Manager, 8, 10, 14, 15, 27, 32, 39, 47, 59, 60, 61, 67, 143
HVT, 7, 10, 15, 18, 50, 99, 143

I

Intelligence Preparation of the Battlefield, v, 2
Interview, 16, 96, 97
IPB, 2, 3, 11, 13, 15, 16, 26, 42, 43, 50, 68, 69, 96, 144

J

Job Title, 20

K

Key terrain, 7, 11, 144

M

Military, 43, 52, 55, 58, 65, 67, 70
Mission, 6, 16, 96, 142

O

Objective, 11, 18, 26, 30, 34, 38, 42, 50, 144
Operations Order, 1
OPORD, 6, 8, 16, 44, 142

P

Pattern, 11, 144
Phase Line, v, 11, 15, 16, 25, 41, 43, 49, 60, 144

R

Recruiter, 15
Resume, 1, 16, 18, 50, 51, 53, 56, 60, 149

S

Sun Tzu, 1, 5, 9, 13, 18, 26, 42, 50, 60, 71, 96

T

Tailor, 16, 50, 53
Target, v, 16, 50, 56
Targeted, 1, 50
Tip, 39, 41
Training, 22, 52, 55, 58, 65, 70

V

VA, 3, 5, 6, 7, 8, 9, 10, 11, 12, 13, 15, 16, 20, 24, 26, 27, 28, 32, 36, 38, 39, 41, 42, 46, 47, 48, 50, 51, 53, 54, 56, 60, 61, 62, 63, 64, 65, 68, 74, 80, 86, 92, 96, 97, 142, 143, 144
Vacancy, 6, 142

W

War, 1, 5, 6, 9, 13, 18, 26, 42, 50, 60, 71, 96, 142
Warning Order, 1, 17, 44
Weapon, 6, 12, 52, 55, 58, 65, 67, 68, 70, 142, 144

ABOUT THE AUTHOR

ABOUT THE AUTHOR

Bruce Benedict is the Owner of Battlefield Résumés, LLC and is a Certified Professional Résumé Writer (CPRW) through The Professional Association of Résumé Writers & Career Coaches as well as a member of The National Résumé Writers' Association. As a Retired U.S. Army Major, Defense Contractor, and a previous Federal Government GS15, he collectively has over 28 years of military, federal government and contracting experience. He has helped clients worldwide and has personal work experiences in Iraq, Afghanistan, Kuwait, Qatar, Bahrain, Japan, Germany and Panama. He has written federal government and defense contracting position descriptions and vacancy announcements, as well as defense contracting statements of work, while interviewing and hiring applicants for the same. Bruce has reviewed thousands of résumés and has developed the Battlefield Résumé Methodology to help veterans leverage their military background so that they can develop a powerful tailored and targeted résumé. Having conducted classified and sensitive work around the world with a high-level security clearance, Bruce understands the sensitivity of operational work and understands how to translate it into a powerful résumé. Bruce also has authored a workbook called "OPERATION: RÉSUMÉ, 4-Battlefield Phases to a Targeted Résumé," which focuses on résumé writing for defense contractor jobs.

Made in the USA
Middletown, DE
29 April 2017